EXAMINATION TEST PA.

Suitable for EDEXCEL EXA

CONTENTS

CORE 1

1. Test Paper 1		1–5
Test Paper 1 Solutions		1–10
2. Test Paper 2		1–4
Test Paper 2 Solutions		1–8
3. Test Paper 3		1–5
Test Paper 3 Solutions		1–7
4. Test Paper 4		1–5
Test Paper 4 Solutions		1–8
5. Test Paper 5		1–4
Test Paper 5 Solutions		1–7
6. Test Paper 6		1–4
Test Paper 6 Solutions		1–7
7. Test Paper 7		1–3
Test Paper 7 Solutions		1–7
8. Test Paper 8		1–4
Test Paper 8 Solutions		1–8
9. Test Paper 9		1–3
Test Paper 9 Solutions		1–6

CORE 2

10.	Test Paper 1	1–4
	Test Paper 1 Solutions	1–8
11.	Test Paper 2	1–4
	Test Paper 2 Solutions	1–9
12.	Test Paper 3	1–4
	Test Paper 3 Solutions	1–9
13.	Test Paper 4	1–4
	Test Paper 4 Solutions	1–7
14.	Test Paper 5	1–5
	Test Paper 5 Solutions	1–7
15.	Test Paper 6	1–5
	Test Paper 6 Solutions	1–7
16.	Test Paper 7	1–4
	Test Paper 7 Solutions	1–10

New impression with corrections made in June 2013

GCE Examinations
Advanced Subsidiary

Test Paper 1

Core Mathematics C1
Time: 1 hour 30 minutes

Instructions and Information

Candidates are not allowed to use calculators for this paper.

Full marks are awarded for answers to ALL questions.

This paper has ten questions.

You can start working with any question and you must label clearly all parts.

1. Solve the equation

   $$x^2 - 6x - 41 = 0,$$

   giving your answers in the form $a + b\sqrt{2}$ where a and b are integers. (3)

   $\dfrac{-b \pm \sqrt{b^2 - 4ac}}{2a}$ $\dfrac{6 \pm \sqrt{36 + 164}}{2} = \dfrac{6 \pm \sqrt{200}}{2} = \dfrac{6 \pm 10\sqrt{2}}{2}$

   $3 + 5\sqrt{2}$ or $3 - 5\sqrt{2}$

2. Find the set of values of x for which

   $$x^2 - 14x > -24.$$ (4)

   $x^2 - 14x + 24 > 0$ $(x - 12)(x - 2) > 0$ $x > 12$ $x > 2$ ✗?

3. The curve with equation $y = f(x)$ passes through the point $(9, 3)$.
   Given that $f'(x) = 5x^{\frac{1}{2}} + 7$
   find $f(x)$. (4)

4. (a) Evaluate $\left(4\tfrac{21}{25}\right)^{-\frac{3}{2}}$. (4)

   (b) Find the value of y such that

   $$\tfrac{1-y}{y} = \sqrt{5},$$

   giving your answer in the form $a + b\sqrt{5}$ where a and b are rational. (4)

5. Given that $f(x) = x^2 + 3x - \dfrac{1}{\sqrt{x}}$

   (a) find $f'(x)$, (3)
   (b) find $\int f(x)\,dx$. (4)

6. $f(x) = -x^{-\frac{1}{2}} + 7x^{\frac{3}{2}}$.

   (a) Evaluate f(5), giving your answer in its simplest form with a rational denominator. **(3)**

   (b) Solve the equation $f(x) = 0$, giving your answer in the form $k\sqrt{7}$. **(4)**

---

7. The straight line l_1 has a gradient of -1 and passes through the point with coordinates $(-2, 3)$.

   (a) Find the equation for l_1 in the general form $ax + by + c = 0$. **(2)**

   The straight line l_2 is perpendicular to the line l_1 and the passes through the point $(1, 2)$.

   (b) Find the equation for l_2 in the form $y = mx + c$. **(3)**

   (c) Find the coordinates of the point of intersection of l_1 and l_2. **(3)**

8.

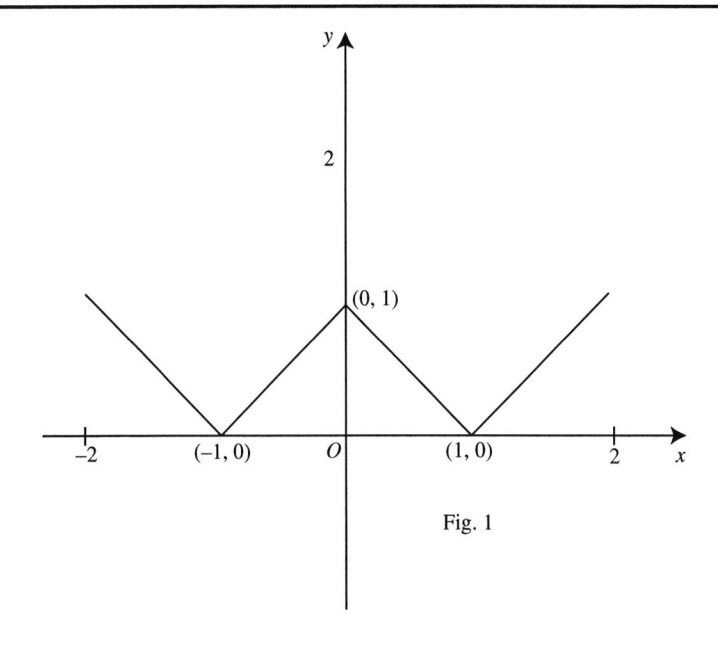

Fig. 1

Fig. 1 Show the graph of $y = f(x)$.

(a) Write down the number of solutions that exist for the equation

    (i) $f(x) = \dfrac{1}{2}$, **(2)**

    (ii) $f(x) = x$. **(1)**

(b) Sketch on separate diagrams the graphs of

    (i) $y = f(x+1)$ **(3)**

    (ii) $y = f\left(\dfrac{1}{2}x\right)$. **(3)**

---

9. (a) Prove that the sum of the first n terms of an arithmetic sequence with the first term 1 and common difference 1 is given by

$$\dfrac{n(n+1)}{2}.$$ **(3)**

(b) Evaluate $5\sum_{r=10}^{50} r$. **(3)**

(c) (i) Find the nth term of the arithmetic series

       25, 23, 21, ... **(2)**

    (ii) Find the number of terms of the series so that the sum becomes negative. **(4)**

---

10. The curve C has the equation

$$y = f(x) \text{ where } f(x) = (x-3)^3.$$

(a) Sketch the curve C, showing the coordinates of any points of intersection with the coordinate axes. **(3)**

(b) Find f'(x).

The straight line l_1 is the tangent of C at the point $P(-1, -64)$. **(3)**

(c) Find the equation for l_1.
The straight line l_2 is parallel to l_1 **(3)**

and is also a tangent to C.

(d) Find the equation of l_2. **(4)**

TOTAL FOR PAPER: 75 MARKS

GCE Examinations
Advanced Subsidiary

Test Paper 1 Solutions

Core Mathematics C1
Time: 1 hour 30 minutes

Instructions and Information

Candidates are not allowed to use calculators for this paper.

Full marks are awarded for answers to ALL questions.

This paper has ten questions.

You can start working with any question and you must label clearly all parts.

1. $x^2 - 6x - 41 = 0$

   applying the quadratic formula
   $$x = \frac{-b \pm \sqrt{b^2 - 4ac}}{2a}$$
   $$x = \frac{-(-6) \pm \sqrt{(-6)^2 - 4(1)(-41)}}{2 \times 1}$$
   $$= \frac{6 \pm \sqrt{36 + 164}}{2}$$
   $$= \frac{6 \pm \sqrt{200}}{2} = \frac{6 \pm 10\sqrt{2}}{2}$$
   $$x = 3 + 5\sqrt{2} \text{ or } x = 3 - 5\sqrt{2}.$$

2. $x^2 - 14x + 24 > 0$

   Look at the constant, $24 = 1 \times 24 = -1 \times -24 = 2 \times 12$
   $$= -2 \times -12 = 6 \times 4 = -6 \times -4$$
   $$= 3 \times 8 = -3 \times -8$$
   $-2 \times -12 = 24.$ $\quad -2 - 12 = -14$
   $\therefore (x^2 - 14x + 24) = (x - 2)(x - 12) > 0$
   $x > 12$ and $x < 2$ are

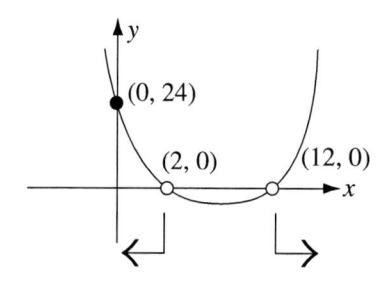

   the set of values of x required.

3. $f(x) = \int f'(x)dx$

$$= \int (5x^{\frac{1}{2}} + 7)dx = \frac{5x^{\frac{3}{2}}}{\frac{3}{2}} + 7x + c$$

$$= \frac{10}{3}x^{\frac{3}{2}} + 7x + c$$

when $x = 9, y = 3 = f(x)$

$$3 = \frac{10}{3}(9)^{\frac{3}{2}} + 7(9) + c$$

$$3 = \frac{10}{3}(3^2)^{\frac{3}{2}} + 63 + c$$

$$= \frac{10}{3}(27) + 63 + c$$

$c = 3 - 63 - 90 = -150$

$\therefore f(x) = \frac{10}{3}x^{\frac{3}{2}} + 7x - 150.$

---

4. (a) $\left(4\frac{21}{25}\right)^{-\frac{3}{2}} = \left(\frac{121}{25}\right)^{-\frac{3}{2}} = \left(\frac{25}{121}\right)^{\frac{3}{2}} = \left(\frac{5}{11}\right)^{3}$

$$= \frac{125}{1331}.$$

(b) $\dfrac{1-y}{y} = \sqrt{5}$

$\dfrac{1}{y} - 1 = \sqrt{5}$

$\dfrac{1}{y} = 1 + \sqrt{5} \Rightarrow y = \dfrac{1}{1+\sqrt{5}}$

$$y = \frac{1}{1+\sqrt{5}} = \frac{1-\sqrt{5}}{(1+\sqrt{5})(1-\sqrt{5})}$$
$$= \frac{1-\sqrt{5}}{1-5} = \frac{1-\sqrt{5}}{-4}$$
$$= -\frac{1}{4} + \frac{1}{4}\sqrt{5}$$

where $a = -\dfrac{1}{4}$ and $b = \dfrac{1}{4}$.

---

5. $f(x) = x^2 + 3x - \dfrac{1}{\sqrt{x}}$

$\qquad = x^2 + 3x - x^{-\frac{1}{2}}$

(a) $f'(x) = 2x + 3 + \dfrac{1}{2}x^{-\frac{3}{2}}$

(b) $\int f(x)dx = \int (x^2 + 3x - x^{-\frac{1}{2}})dx$

$$= \frac{x^3}{3} + \frac{3x^2}{2} - \frac{x^{\frac{1}{2}}}{\frac{1}{2}} + c$$

$$= \frac{x^3}{3} + \frac{3x^2}{2} - 2x^{\frac{1}{2}} + c$$

$$= \frac{x^3}{3} + \frac{3x^2}{2} - 2\sqrt{x} + c.$$

---

6. (a) $f(x) = -x^{-\frac{1}{2}} + 7x^{\frac{3}{2}}$

$f(5) = -5^{-\frac{1}{2}} + 7(5^{\frac{3}{2}})$

$\qquad = -\dfrac{1}{\sqrt{5}} + 7 \times 5\sqrt{5}$

$\qquad = -\dfrac{1}{\sqrt{5}} + 35\sqrt{5} = -\dfrac{1}{\sqrt{5}} + \dfrac{35\sqrt{5}\sqrt{5}}{\sqrt{5}}$

$$f(5) = \frac{-1 + 175}{\sqrt{5}} = \frac{174}{\sqrt{5}} \times \frac{\sqrt{5}}{\sqrt{5}}$$

$$= \frac{174}{5}\sqrt{5}.$$

(b) $-x^{-\frac{1}{2}} + 7x^{\frac{3}{2}} = 0$

$7x^{\frac{3}{2}} = \frac{1}{\sqrt{x}}$

$x^2 = \frac{1}{7}$

$x = \pm\frac{1}{\sqrt{7}}$

$x = \frac{1}{\sqrt{7}} \times \frac{\sqrt{7}}{\sqrt{7}} = \frac{1}{7}\sqrt{7}$ where $k = \frac{1}{7}$

$x = -\frac{1}{\sqrt{7}} \times \frac{\sqrt{7}}{\sqrt{7}} = -\frac{1}{7}\sqrt{7}$ where $k = -\frac{1}{7}$.

---

7. (a)

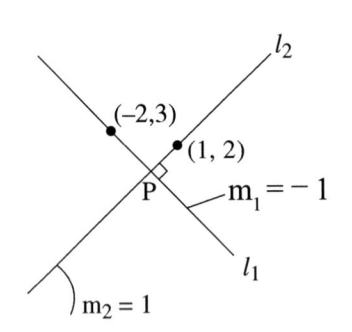

$y = mx + c$

$y = -x + c$

$3 = -(-2) + c$

$c = 3 - 2 = 1$

$y = -x + 1$

$\boxed{x + y - 1 = 0}$

(b) $m_1 m_2 = -1$ for two lines that are perpendicular

if $m_1 = -1$, $m_2 = \dfrac{-1}{-1} = 1$

$y = mx + c$

$y = x + c$

$2 = 1 + c$

$c = 1$

$\boxed{y = x + 1}$

(c) $y = -x + 1$ ...(1)

$y = x + 1$ ...(2)

adding (1) and (2)

$2y = 2$

$\boxed{y = 1}$

$\boxed{x = 0}$

$\therefore P(0, 1)$.

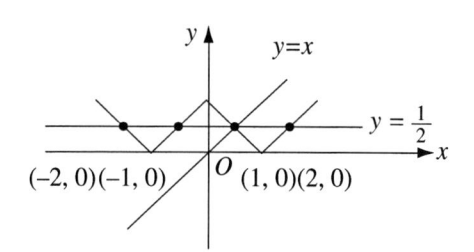

(a) (i) $f(x) = \dfrac{1}{2}$

4 solutions.

(ii) 1 solution.

(b) (i)

Graph of $f(x+1)$ with points $(-3, 0)$, $(-2, 0)$, $(-1, 1)$, $(1, 0)$.

Graph of $f(\frac{1}{2}x)$ with points $(-2, 0)$, $(0, 1)$, $(2, 0)$.

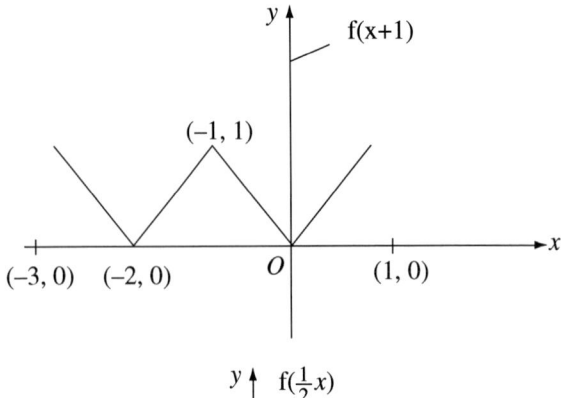

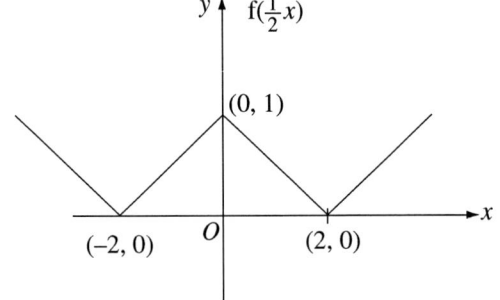

---

9. (a) $1, 2, 3, 4, \ldots n$

$S_n = 1 + 2 + 3 + 4 + \ldots + n \ldots(1)$

$S_n = n + (n-1) + (n-2) + \ldots + 1 \ldots(2)$

adding (1) and (2)

$2S_n = (1+n) + (1+n) + (1+n) + \ldots n$ times

$$\boxed{S_n = \frac{n(n+1)}{2}}$$

(b) $5\sum_{r=1}^{50} r = 5\sum_{r=1}^{9} r + 5\sum_{r=10}^{50} r$

$5 \times \dfrac{50 \times 51}{2} = 5 \times \dfrac{9 \times 10}{2} + 5\sum_{r=10}^{50} r$

$5\sum_{r=10}^{50} r = 5 \times 25 \times 51 - 5 \times 9 \times 5$

$\qquad = 125 \times 51 - 25 \times 9 = 6375 - 225 = 6150$

$$\begin{array}{r} 125 \\ \underline{51\times} \\ 125 \\ \underline{625} \\ 6375 \end{array}$$

(c) (i) $T_n = a + (n-1)d$

$\qquad = 25 + (n-1)(-2)$

$\qquad = 25 - 2n + 2$

$\qquad = 27 - 2n$

$S_n = \dfrac{n}{2}[2a + (n-1)d] < 0$

$25n + \dfrac{n}{2}(n-1)(-2) < 0$

$25n + n(n-1)(-1) < 0$

$25n - n^2 + n < 0$

$26n - n^2 < 0$

$n(26 - n) < 0$

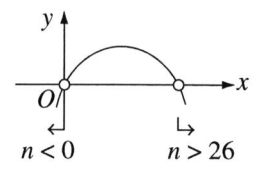

$n < 0 \qquad n > 26$

We cannot have negative term so $n > 26$, the sum becomes negative.

10. (a) $f(x) = x^3$

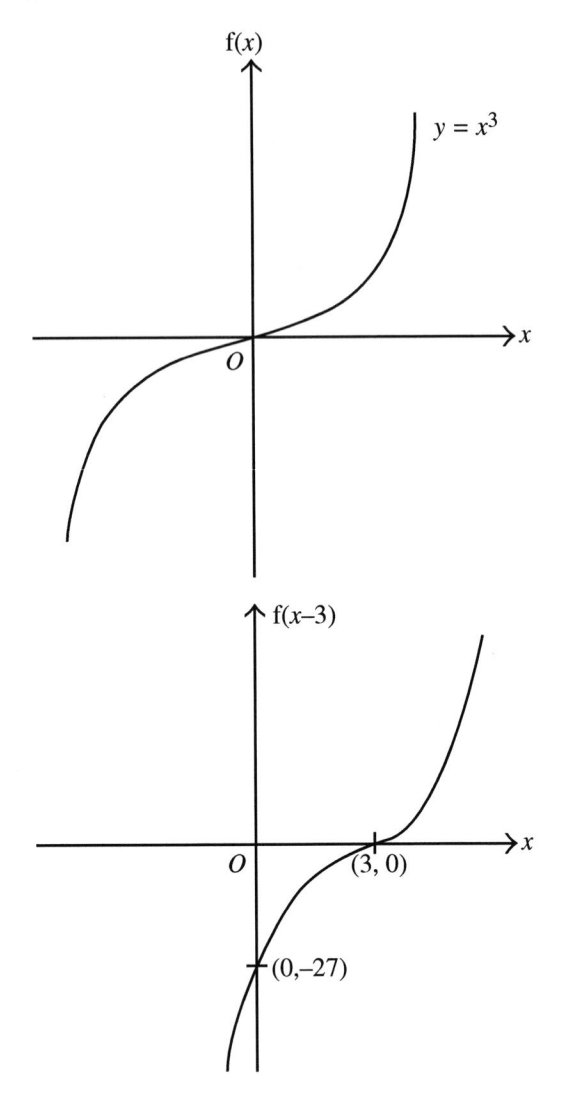

[Graph of $y = x^3$]

[Graph of $f(x-3)$ showing points $(3, 0)$ and $(0, -27)$]

when $x = 0$

$y = (-3)^3 = -27$.

(b) $f'(x) = 3(x-3)^2 = 3(x^2 - 6x + 9) = 3x^2 - 18x + 27$
or $f(x) = (x-3)^3 = (x-3)(x^2 - 6x + 9)$
$= x^3 - 6x^2 + 9x - 3x^2 + 18x - 27$
$= x^3 - 9x^2 + 27x - 27$
$f'(x) = 3x^2 - 18x + 27$

(c) $f'(-1)$ is the gradient at $x = -1$
$f'(-1) = 3(-1)^2 - 18(-1) + 27 = 3 + 18 + 27$
$= 48$
$y = 48x + c \qquad -64 = 48(-1) + c \Rightarrow c = -16$
$y = 48x - 16.$

(d) l_2 has the same gradient as l_1 since they are parallel.
$3x^2 - 18x + 27 = 48$
$3x^2 - 18x - 21 = 0$
$x^2 - 6x - 7 = 0$
$(x-7)(x+1) = 0$
$x - 1$ or $x = 7$
when $x = 7$, $y = (7-3)^3 = 64$
$(7, 64)$
$y = 48x + c$
$64 = 48 \times 7 + c$
$c = 64 - 336 = -272$
$y = 48x - 272.$

GCE Examinations
Advanced Subsidiary

Test Paper 2

Core Mathematics C1
Time: 1 hour 30 minutes

Instructions and Information

Candidates are not allowed to use calculators for this paper.

Full marks are awarded for answers to ALL questions.

This paper has ten questions.

You can start working with any question and you must label clearly all parts.

1. The roots of a quadratic equation are $x = 3 \pm 5\sqrt{2}$.
   Show that the quadratic equation is $x^2 - 6x - 41 = 0$. (4)

2. Find the set of values of x for which $x^2 + 25x + 24 < 0$. (4)

3. The curve with equation $y = f(x)$ passes through the point $(25, 1)$.
   Given that $f'(x) = 3x^{-\frac{1}{2}} - 4$ find $f(x)$. (6)

4. (a) Evaluate $\left(3\frac{1}{16}\right)^{-\frac{1}{2}}$. (3)

   (b) Find the value of t such that $\frac{5-t}{t} = \sqrt{7}$,
   giving your answer in the form $a + b\sqrt{7}$ where a and b are rational. (4)

5. Given that $f(x) = -x^3 - 2x^2 + x + \frac{1}{\sqrt{x^3}}$,

   (a) find $f'(x)$, (3)
   (b) $\int f(x) dx$. (4)

6. $f(x) = x^{-\frac{1}{2}} - 3x^{\frac{3}{2}}$.

   (a) Evaluate $f(2)$, giving your answer in its simplest form with a rational denominator. (3)

   (b) Solve the equation $f(x) = 0$ giving your answers in the form $k\sqrt{3}$. (4)

7. The straight line l_1 has a gradient of 2 and passes through the point with coordinates $(2, -3)$.

   (a) Find the equation for l_1 in the intercept form $\frac{x}{a} + \frac{y}{b} = 1$. (2)

   The straight line l_2 is perpendicular to the line l_1 and passes through the point $(-1, 2)$.

   (b) Find the equation for l_2 in the form $ax + by + c = 0$. (3)

   (c) Find the coordinates of the point of intersection of l_1 and l_2. (3)

8.

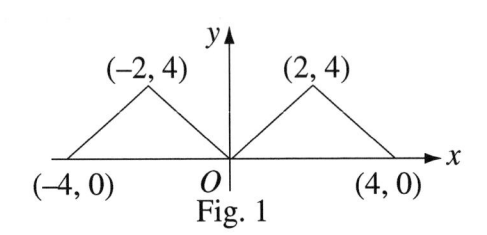

Fig. 1

Fig. 1 shows the graphs of $y = f(x)$.

   (a) Write down the number of solutions that exist for the equation

   (i) $f(x) = 2$ (1)

   (ii) $f(x) = -x$. (1)

   (b) Sketch on separate diagrams the graphs of

   (i) $y = f(x - 2)$ (3)

   (ii) $y = f(2x)$. (3)

9. (a) An arithmetic sequence has a first term $a = \frac{3}{2}$ and a common difference $d = \frac{1}{2}$.

   (i) Deduce that the nth term is $T_n = 1 + \frac{1}{2}n$ and show that

   (ii) the sum of n terms is $\frac{5n}{4} + \frac{n^2}{4}$. (3)

(b) Evaluate $\sum_{r=1}^{100}(2r-1)$. (2)

(c) Florence every year saves money in a bank account, the first year she saves £100 and she increases that amount by £100 every year. How much money has she put away in 20 years. (6)

10. The curve C has the equation

$$y = f(x) \text{ where } f(x) = (x+1)^3.$$

(a) Sketch the curve C, showing the coordinates of any points of intersection with the coordinate axes. (3)

(b) Find $f'(x)$. (3)

The straight line l_1 is the tangent to C at the point $P(1, 8)$.

(c) Find the equation for l_1. (3)

The straight line l_2 is parallel to l_1 and is also a tangent to C.

(d) Find the equation of l_2. (4)

TOTAL FOR PAPER: 75 MARKS

GCE Examinations
Advanced Subsidiary

Test Paper 2 Solutions

Core Mathematics C1
Time: 1 hour 30 minutes

Instructions and Information

Candidates are not allowed to use calculators for this paper.

Full marks are awarded for answers to ALL questions.

This paper has ten questions.

You can start working with any question and you must label clearly all parts.

1. $x = 3 + 5\sqrt{2} \Rightarrow x - 3 - 5\sqrt{2} = 0$
   $x = 3 - 5\sqrt{2} \Rightarrow x - 3 + 5\sqrt{2} = 0$.
   The quadratic equation is $(x - 3 - 5\sqrt{2})(x - 3 + 5\sqrt{2}) = 0$
   $(x - 3)^2 - (5\sqrt{2})^2 = 0$
   $x^2 - 6x + 9 - 50 = 0$
   $\therefore \boxed{x^2 - 6x - 41 = 0}$

---

2. $x^2 + 25x + 24 < 0$
   $(x + 24)(x + 1) < 0$

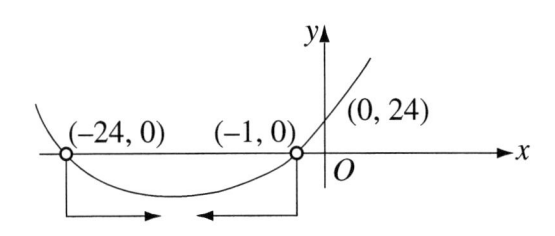

   $-24 < x < -1$.

---

3. $f(x) = \int f'(x)dx = \int (3x^{-\frac{1}{2}} - 4)dx$
   $f(x) = \frac{3x^{\frac{1}{2}}}{\frac{1}{2}} - 4x + c$
   $f(x) = 6x^{\frac{1}{2}} - 4x + c$
   $1 = 6(25)^{\frac{1}{2}} - 4(25) + c$
   $c = 1 - 6 \times 5 + 100 = 71$
   $f(x) = 6\sqrt{x} - 4x + 71$.

---

4. (a) $(3\frac{1}{16})^{-\frac{1}{2}} = \left(\frac{49}{16}\right)^{-\frac{1}{2}} = \left(\frac{16}{49}\right)^{\frac{1}{2}} = \frac{4}{7}$.

(b) $\frac{5-t}{t} = \sqrt{7}$

$\frac{5}{t} - 1 = \sqrt{7}$

$\frac{5}{t} = 1 + \sqrt{7}$

$\frac{t}{5} = \frac{1}{1+\sqrt{7}} \times \frac{1-\sqrt{7}}{1-\sqrt{7}} = \frac{1-\sqrt{7}}{1-7}$

$t = \frac{5}{6}(\sqrt{7} - 1) = -\frac{5}{6} + \frac{5}{6}\sqrt{7}$

$a = -\frac{5}{6}$ and $b = \frac{5}{6}$.

---

5. $f(x) = -x^3 - 2x^2 + x + \frac{1}{\sqrt{x^3}}$

   $f(x) = -x^3 - 2x^2 + x + x^{-\frac{3}{2}}$

   (a) $f'(x) = -3x^2 - 4x + 1 - \frac{3}{2}x^{-\frac{5}{2}}$

   (b) $\int f(x)dx = \int (-x^3 - 2x^2 + x + x^{-\frac{3}{2}})dx$

   $= -\frac{x^4}{4} - \frac{2x^3}{3} + \frac{x^2}{2} + \frac{x^{-\frac{1}{2}}}{-\frac{1}{2}} + c$

   $= -\frac{x^4}{4} - \frac{2x^3}{3} + \frac{x^2}{2} - \frac{2}{\sqrt{x}} + c.$

---

6. (a) $f(x) = x^{-\frac{1}{2}} - 3x^{\frac{3}{2}}$

   $f(2) = 2^{-\frac{1}{2}} - 3(2)^{\frac{3}{2}}$

   $= \frac{1}{\sqrt{2}} - \frac{3 \times 2\sqrt{2} \times \sqrt{2}}{\sqrt{2}}$

   $= \frac{1 - 6 \times 2}{\sqrt{2}}$

   $= -\frac{11}{\sqrt{2}} = \frac{-11\sqrt{2}}{\sqrt{2}\sqrt{2}} = -\frac{11}{2}\sqrt{2}.$

(b) $x^{-\frac{1}{2}} - 3x^{\frac{3}{2}} = 0$

$3x^{\frac{3}{2}} = \frac{1}{x^{\frac{1}{2}}}$

$3x^2 = 1$

$x^2 = \frac{1}{3}$

$x = \pm\frac{1}{\sqrt{3}} = \pm\frac{\sqrt{3}}{3}$

where $k = \pm\frac{1}{3}$.

---

7. (a) $y = 2x + c$

$-3 = 2(2) + c$

$c = -7$

$y = 2x - 7$

$y - 2x = -7$

$\boxed{\dfrac{y}{-7} + \dfrac{x}{\frac{7}{2}} = 1}$

(b) The gradient of l_2 is given

$m_1 m_2 = -1 \Rightarrow m_2 = -\frac{1}{2}$

$y = -\frac{1}{2}x + c$

$2 = -\frac{1}{2}(-1) + c$

$c = 2 - \frac{1}{2} = \frac{3}{2}$

$y = -\frac{1}{2}x + \frac{3}{2}$

$\boxed{x + 2y - 3 = 0}$

(c) $y - 2x = -7 \ldots (1)$

$\underline{y + \frac{1}{2}x = \frac{3}{2} \ldots (2) \times 4}$

$y - 2x = -7 \ldots (3)$

$\underline{4y + 2x = 6 \ldots (4)}$

$(3) + (4)\ 5y = -1$

$\boxed{y = -\frac{1}{5}}$

Substitute in (1)

$-\frac{1}{5} - 2x = -7$

$-2x = -7 + \frac{1}{5} = -\frac{34}{5}$

$x = \frac{34}{10} = 3\frac{2}{5}$.

$\therefore P\left(3\frac{2}{5}, -\frac{1}{5}\right).$

---

8. (a) (i) 4 points

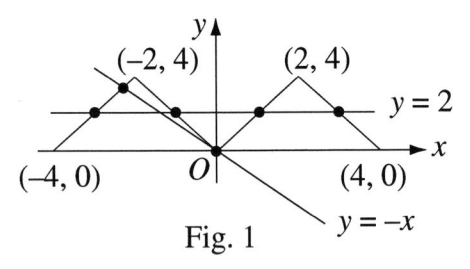

Fig. 1

(ii) 2 points.

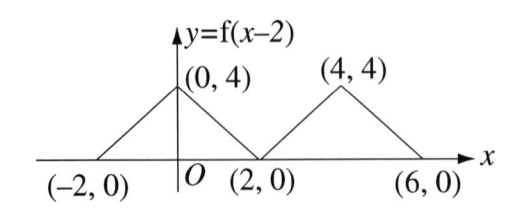

(b) (i)

(ii)

$y = f(2x)$ graph with peaks at $(-1, 4)$ and $(1, 4)$, base points at $(-2, 0)$ and $(2, 0)$.

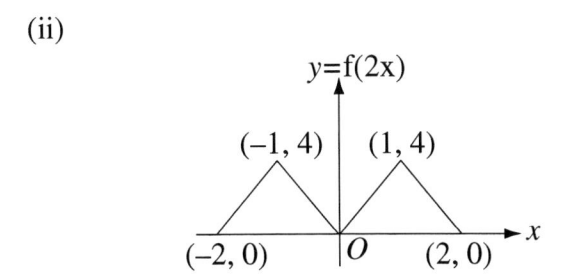

9. (a) (i) $\frac{3}{2}, \frac{3}{2} + \frac{1}{2}, \frac{3}{2} + 2\left(\frac{1}{2}\right) \ldots \frac{3}{2} + (n-1)\frac{1}{2}$

$\quad\quad$ 1st $\quad$ 2nd $\quad\quad$ 3rd $\quad\quad\quad\quad$ n^{th}

$\quad\quad T_n = \frac{3}{2} + (n-1)\frac{1}{2} = \frac{3}{2} + \frac{1}{2}n - \frac{1}{2} = 1 + \frac{1}{2}n.$

$\quad$ (ii) $S_n = \frac{n}{2}[2a + (n-1)d]$

$\quad\quad\quad = \frac{n}{2}[a + T_n] = \frac{n}{2}\left[\frac{3}{2} + 1 + \frac{1}{2}n\right]$

$\quad\quad\quad \boxed{S_n = \frac{5}{4}n + \frac{n^2}{4}}.$

(b) $\sum_{r=1}^{100}(2r - 1) = 2\sum_{r=1}^{100} r - \sum_{r=1}^{100} 1$

$\quad\quad\quad\quad\quad\quad\quad = 2 \times \frac{100 \times 101}{2} - 100$

$\quad\quad\quad\quad\quad\quad\quad = 10100 - 100$

$\quad\quad\quad\quad\quad\quad\quad = 10000.$

(c) $100 + (100 + 100) + (100 + 200) + \ldots 100 + 19 \times 100$

$\quad 100 + 200 + 300 + \ldots 2000$

$\quad S_n = \frac{n}{2}[a + T_n]$

$\quad S_{20} = \frac{20}{2}[100 + 2000] = £21000.$

10. (a)

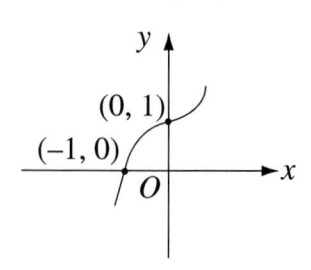

A graph showing a curve passing through $(-1, 0)$ and $(0, 1)$.

(b) $f(x) = (x+1)^3 = x^3 + 3x^2 + 3x + 1$
$ = (x+1)(x+1)^2 = (x+1)(x^2+2x+1)$
$ = x^3 + x^2 + 2x^2 + 2x + x + 1$
$ = x^3 + 3x^2 + 3x + 1$
$f'(x) = 3x^2 + 6x + 3.$

(c) The gradient at $x = 1$
$f'(1) = 3 + 6 + 3 = 12$
$y = 12x + c$
$8 = 12(1) + c$
$c = -4$
$\boxed{y = 12x - 4}$

(d) $3x^2 + 6x + 3 = 12$ the gradient of l_2 is the same as that of l_1
$3x^2 + 6x - 9 = 0$
$x^2 + 2x - 3 = 0$
$(x+3)(x-1) = 0$

$$x = 1 \quad \text{or} \quad x = -3$$

when $x = -3$ $y = f(-3) = -8$
$y = 12x + c$
$-8 = 12(-3) + c$
$c = -8 + 36 = 28$
$$\boxed{y = 12x + 28}$$

TOTAL FOR PAPER: 75 MARKS

GCE Examinations
Advanced Subsidiary

Test Paper 3

Core Mathematics C1
Time: 1 hour 30 minutes

Instructions and Information

Candidates are not allowed to use calculators for this paper.

Full marks are awarded for answers to ALL questions.

This paper has ten questions.

You can start working with any question and you must label clearly all parts.

1. A straight line has a gradient of -3 and passes through the point $(4, 5)$. Determine the equation of the line in the form:

   (i) $y = mx + c$ (2)

   (ii) $ax + by + c = 0$ (1)

   (iii) $\frac{x}{a} + \frac{y}{b} = 1$. (2)

---

2. (a) Factorise $x^2 - 8x + 15$. (2)

   (b) Find the set of value of x that satisfy the inequality
   $x^2 - 8x + 15 \leq 0$. (3)

---

3. (a) Solve the simultaneous equations
   $$x^2 + y^2 = 4 \quad \ldots (1)$$
   $$-x + y = 2 \quad \ldots (2)$$ (5)

   (b) Sketch the graphs for (1) and (2) and indicate the solutions.

---

4. (a) If $\frac{1-\sqrt{2}}{1+\sqrt{2}} = a + b\sqrt{2}$ find a and b. (2)

   (b) Evaluate $\left(5\frac{1}{16}\right)^{-\frac{3}{2}}$. (2)

---

5. (a) Sketch the graphs $y = x^2$ and $y^2 = x$, and find the coordinates of the points of intersection. (5)

   (b) Determine the area enclosed between the curves. (5)

---

6. (a) Sketch the curve $y = x^3$. (2)

   (b) Find the gradient at the point $x = 2$. (2)

   (c) Find the equation of the tangent at $x = 2$. (4)

(d) Determine the coordinates of the point Q where the tangent has the same gradient as at P. (2)

(e) Find the equation of the normal at Q in the form $ax + by + c = 0$. (4)

---

7. Given that $f(x) = x^{\frac{3}{2}} - x^{-\frac{1}{2}}$

   (a) find $f'(x)$, (3)
   (b) $\int f(x)\,dx$. (4)

---

8. The nth term of an arithmetic sequence is $5(n+1)$. Find the sum of 25 terms. (4)

---

9. If $f(x) = x^2$ sketch the graphs (i) $f(2x)$ (ii) $f(x) + 2$. (4)

---

10. (a) If $f(x) = 2x^2 - 4x + 3 = a(x+b)^2 + c$.
    Determine the values of a, b and c. (2)

    (b) Sketch the graph, indicating the coordinates of the point of intersection of the curve and the y-axis. (2)

    (c) Evaluate the coordinates of the minimum point, explaining the reason. (4)

    (d) Determine the discriminant.
    What does this indicate? (2)

    (e) Find the roots of $f(x) - 1 = 0$. (2)

TOTAL FOR PAPER: 75 MARKS

GCE Examinations
Advanced Subsidiary

Test Paper 3 Solutions

Core Mathematics C1
Time: 1 hour 30 minutes

Instructions and Information

Candidates are not allowed to use calculators for this paper.

Full marks are awarded for answers to ALL questions.

This paper has ten questions.

You can start working with any question and you must label clearly all parts.

1. (i) $y = mx + c = -3x + c \Rightarrow 5 = -3(4) + c \Rightarrow c = 17$

   $\therefore \boxed{y = -3x + 17}$ the gradient/intercept form

   (ii) $\boxed{3x + y - 17 = 0}$ the general form

   (iii) $3x + y = 17$

   $\frac{3x}{17} + \frac{y}{17} = 1$

   $\boxed{\frac{x}{\frac{17}{3}} + \frac{y}{17} = 1}$ where $a = \frac{17}{3}, b = 17$

   the intercept form.

---

2. (a) $x^2 - 8x + 15 = (x - 3)(x - 5)$.

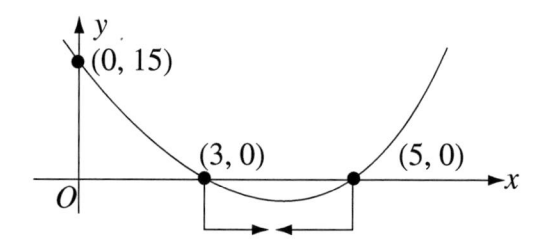

   (b) $(x - 3)(x - 5) \leq 0$.

   The set of values of x that satisfy the inequality is $3 \leq x \leq 5$.

---

3. (a) From (2), we have

   $-x + y = 2 \Rightarrow y = x + 2$ substituting into (1), we have
   $x^2 + y^2 = x^2 + (x+2)^2 = x^2 + x^2 + 4x + 4$
   $\qquad = 2x^2 + 4x + 4 = 4$
   $2x^2 + 4x = 0$
   $2x(x + 2) = 0$
   $x = 0, \quad x = -2$
   $y = 2, \quad y = 0$.

(b)

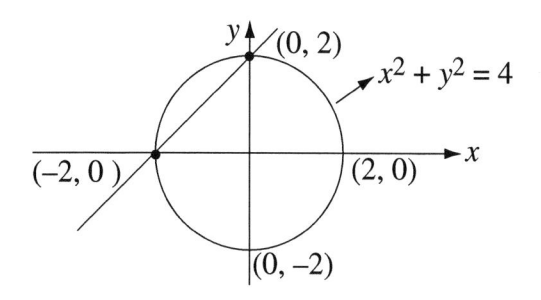

4. (a) $\frac{1-\sqrt{2}}{1+\sqrt{2}} = \frac{(1-\sqrt{2})(1-\sqrt{2})}{(1+\sqrt{2})(1-\sqrt{2})} = \frac{1-2\sqrt{2}+2}{1-2} = -3+2\sqrt{2}$

$a = -3$ and $b = 2$.

(b) $\left(5\frac{1}{16}\right)^{-\frac{3}{2}} = \left(\frac{81}{16}\right)^{-\frac{3}{2}} = \left(\frac{16}{81}\right)^{\frac{3}{2}} = \left(\frac{4}{9}\right)^{3} = \frac{64}{729}$.

5. (a)

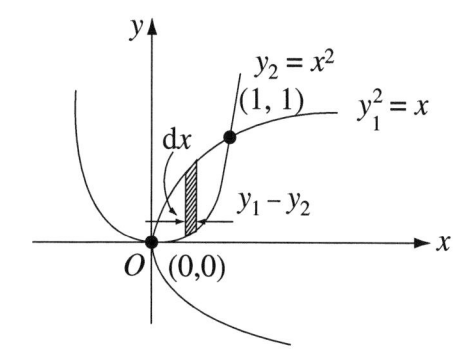

Squaring both sides of $y = x^2$

$y^2 = x^4 = x \Rightarrow x^4 - x = 0 \Rightarrow x(x^3 - 1) = 0$

$x = 0$ or $x = 1$.

When $x = 0$, $y = 0$; when $x = 1$, $y = 1$.

(b) The elemental area of the strip is $(y_1 - y_2)dx$

$\int_0^1 (y_1 - y_2)dx = \int_0^1 (\sqrt{x} - x^2)dx = \int_0^1 (x^{\frac{1}{2}} - x^2)dx$

$= \left[\dfrac{x^{\frac{3}{2}}}{\frac{3}{2}} - \dfrac{x^3}{3}\right]_0^1 = \dfrac{2}{3} - \dfrac{1}{3} = \dfrac{1}{3}$ s.u.

---

6. (a)

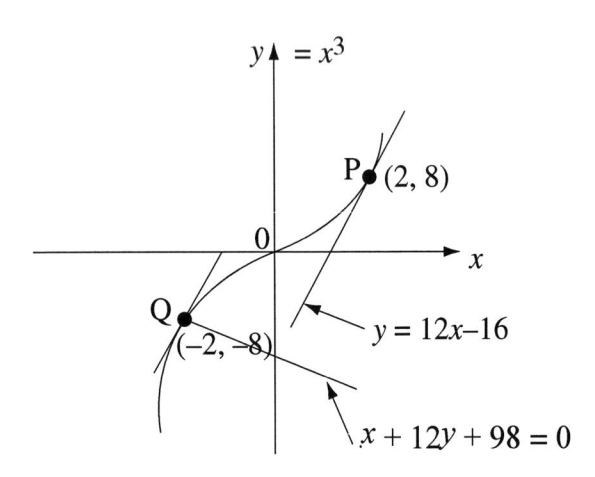

(b) $y = x^3$

$\dfrac{dy}{dx} = 3x^2$

when $x = 2$, $\dfrac{dy}{dx} = 12$.

(c) $y = mx + c$

$y = 12x + c$

when $x = 2$, $y = 8$

$8 = 12(2) + c \Rightarrow c = 8 - 24 = -16$

$\therefore \boxed{y = 12x - 16}$.

(d) when $x = -2$ $\frac{dy}{dx} = 3(-2)^2 = 12$ the gradient is the same

(e) $m_1 = 12$, $m_2 = -\frac{1}{12}$.

The equation of the normal at Q

$y = -\frac{1}{12}x + c$

$-8 = -\frac{1}{12}(-2) + c \Rightarrow -8 - \frac{1}{6} = c = -\frac{49}{6}$

$y = -\frac{1}{12}x - \frac{49}{6} \Rightarrow \boxed{x + 12y + 98 = 0}$

---

7. (a) $f(x) = x^{\frac{3}{2}} - x^{-\frac{1}{2}}$

$f'(x) = \frac{3}{2}x^{\frac{1}{2}} + \frac{1}{2}x^{-\frac{3}{2}}$

(b) $\int \left(x^{\frac{3}{2}} - x^{-\frac{1}{2}}\right) dx = \frac{x^{\frac{5}{2}}}{\frac{5}{2}} - \frac{x^{\frac{1}{2}}}{\frac{1}{2}} + c$

$= \frac{2}{5}x^{\frac{5}{2}} - 2x^{\frac{1}{2}} + c.$

---

8. $5(1+1), 5(2+1), 5(3+1), \ldots \quad 5(n+1)$

$10, 15, 20, \ldots 5(n+1)$

$S_n = \frac{n}{2}[2a + (n-1)d]$

$S_n = \frac{25}{2}[2 \times 10 + 24 \times 5]$

$= 25(10 + 60)$

$= 25 \times 70 = 1750.$

9.

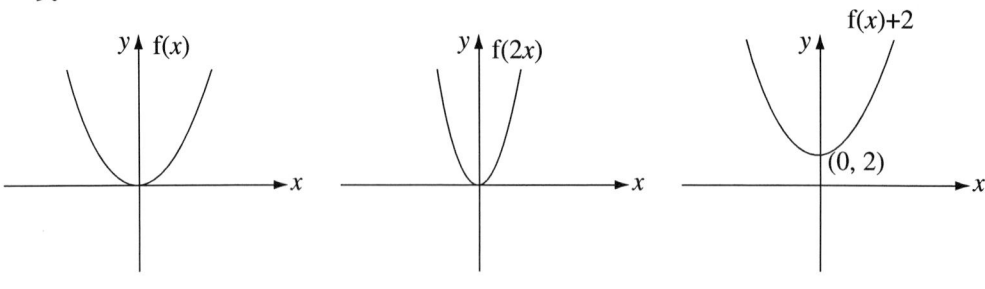

[Three graphs shown: f(x), f(2x), and f(x)+2 with point (0, 2)]

10. (a) $2x^2 - 4x + 3 \equiv a(x+b)^2 + c$

$2x^2 - 4x + 3 \equiv a(x^2 + 2bx + b^2) + c$

$2x^2 - 4x + 3 \equiv ax^2 + 2abx + ab^2 + c$.

Equating coefficients

$\boxed{a = 2}$, $2ab = -4$, $3 = ab^2 + c$

$\boxed{b = -1}$ $3 = 2(-1)^2 + c \Rightarrow \boxed{c = 1}$

$\therefore 2x^2 - 4x + 3 \equiv 2(x-1)^2 + 1$.

(b) When $x = 0$, $y = 3$; (0, 3) the point of intersection of the curve and the y-axis.

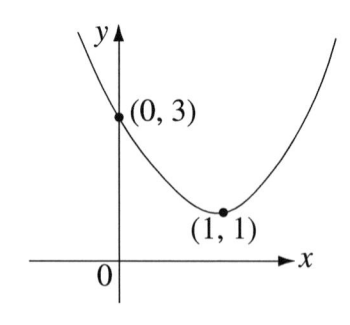

[Graph shown with points (0, 3) and (1, 1)]

(c) The coordinates of the minimum point are (1,1), since $(x-1)^2$ is always positive except when $x = 1$ is zero

$f(x) = 2(x-1)^2 + 1$

$f(1) = 1.$

(d) $D = b^2 - 4ac = (-4)^2 - 4(2)(3) = 16 - 24 = -8.$ The discriminant is negative and indicates that the curve neither intersect nor touches the x-axis.

(e) $f(x) - 1 = 2(x-1)^2 + 1 - 1 = 2(x-1)^2 = 0 \quad x = 1$ twice the curve touches the x-axis.

TOTAL FOR PAPER: 75 MARKS

GCE Examinations
Advanced Subsidiary

Test Paper 4

Core Mathematics C1
Time: 1 hour 30 minutes

Instructions and Information

Candidates are not allowed to use calculators for this paper.

Full marks are awarded for answers to ALL questions.

This paper has ten questions.

You can start working with any question and you must label clearly all parts.

1. Evaluate:

   (i) $\sum_{r=1}^{1000} r$ (2)

   (ii) $\sum_{r=501}^{1000} r$. (3)

2. If $\dfrac{\sqrt{3}-\sqrt{2}}{\sqrt{3}+\sqrt{2}} = a + b\sqrt{6}$

   find a and b. (3)

3. (a) $x^2 - 5x - 9 \equiv (x+a)^2 + b$.
   Find a and b and hence sketch the graph indicating the coordinates of the points of intersections with the axes. (3)

   (b) Determine the coordinates of the minimum point. (3)

4. (a) Sketch the graph of $y = f(x) = -x^3$. (1)

   (b) Sketch
   (i) $f(-x)$ (2)
   (ii) $f(2x)$. (2)

5. The quadratic function f(x) is shown in Fig. 1.

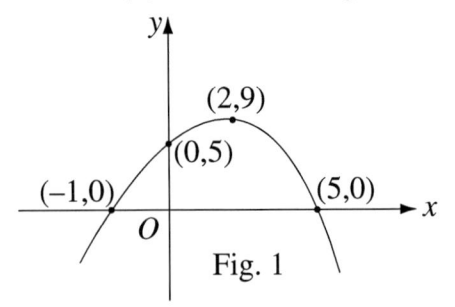

Fig. 1

Determine the quadratic expressive f(x). **(6)**

---

6. (a) A straight line intersects the axes at $(0, 5)$ and $(-4, 0)$, find the equation of the line in the form $ax + by + c = 0$. **(3)**

(b) Show that the point $P\left(-3, \frac{5}{4}\right)$ lies on the line. **(3)**

(c) Find the equation of the perpendicular line passing through P, in the form $ax + by + c = 0$. **(4)**

---

7. Fig. 2. shows a quadratic function $f(x)$; $y = f(x) = -x^2 + 2x + 3$

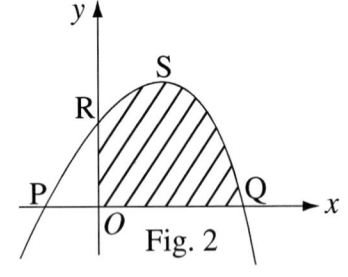

Fig. 2

(a) Factorise $f(x)$. **(3)**
(b) Determine the coordinates of P, R and Q. **(2)**
(c) Find the area under the graph in the positive quadrant. **(3)**
(d) Determine the coordinates of the maximum point. **(4)**

8.

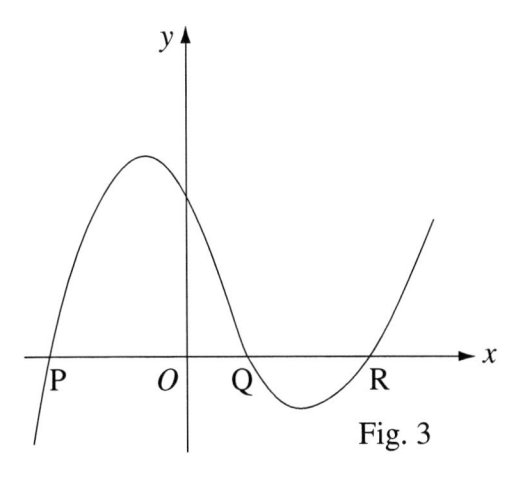

Fig. 3

Fig. 3 shows part of the curve C with equation $y = (x - 2)(x^2 - 9)$.

The curve cuts the x-axis at the points P, Q and R, as shown in Fig. 3.

(a) Write down the coordinates of P, Q and R. (3)

(b) Show that $\frac{dy}{dx} = 3x^2 - 4x - 9$. (3)

(c) Find the equation of the tangent to C at $S(-2, 20)$. (4)

(d) Find the exact coordinates at the point when the tangent to C is parallel to the tangent at S. (4)

---

9. The first three terms of an arithmetic progression are a, b and c. Determine:

(i) The common difference (1)

(ii) The arithmetic mean (2)

(iii) The nth term (3)

(iv) The sum of n terms. (4)

10. (a) if $y = f(x) = \frac{3}{\sqrt{x}} - \frac{5}{x^2} + \frac{7}{x^3} + 9$ determine the first derivative and hence evaluate $f'(1)$ as a rational fraction. (3)

(b) The gradient of a curve is given but the differential equation.
$$\frac{dy}{dx} = 3x^{\frac{1}{2}}$$
determine the general equation of the curve and the particular equation of the curve when the curve passes through the point $(1, 0)$. (6)

TOTAL FOR PAPER: 75 MARKS

GCE Examinations
Advanced Subsidiary

Test Paper 4 Solutions

Core Mathematics C1
Time: 1 hour 30 minutes

Instructions and Information

Candidates are not allowed to use calculators for this paper.

Full marks are awarded for answers to ALL questions.

This paper has ten questions.

You can start working with any question and you must label clearly all parts.

1. (i) $\sum_{r=1}^{1000} r = \frac{1000 \times 1001}{2} = 500 \times 1001 = 500\,500.$

(ii) $\sum_{r=1}^{1000} r = \sum_{r=1}^{500} r + \sum_{r=501}^{1000} r.$

$\sum_{r=501}^{1000} r = \sum_{r=1}^{1000} r - \sum_{r=1}^{500} r$

$= \frac{1000 \times 1001}{2} - \frac{500 \times 501}{2}$

$= 500\,500 - 250 \times 501$

$= 500\,500 - 125\,250$

$= 375\,250.$

2. $\frac{\sqrt{3}-\sqrt{2}}{\sqrt{3}+\sqrt{2}} = \frac{\sqrt{3}-\sqrt{2}}{\sqrt{3}+\sqrt{2}} \times \frac{\sqrt{3}-\sqrt{2}}{\sqrt{3}-\sqrt{2}} = \frac{3-2\sqrt{2}\sqrt{3}+2}{3-2}$

$= 5 - 2\sqrt{2}\sqrt{3} = 5 - 2\sqrt{6}$

$a = 5, \quad b = -2.$

3. (a) $x^2 - 5x - 9 \equiv (x+a)^2 + b$

$x^2 - 5x - 9 \equiv x^2 + 2ax + a^2 + b$

equating coefficients

$2a = -5 \Rightarrow a = -\frac{5}{2}$

$-9 = a^2 + b \Rightarrow -9 = \frac{25}{4} + b \Rightarrow b = -\frac{36}{4} - \frac{25}{4}$

$b = -\frac{61}{4}$

$\therefore x^2 - 5x - 9 \equiv \left(x - \frac{5}{2}\right)^2 - \frac{61}{4}.$

If $x^2 - 5x - 9 = 0$

$$\left(x - \tfrac{5}{2}\right)^2 - \tfrac{61}{4} = 0$$
$$\left(x - \tfrac{5}{2}\right)^2 = \tfrac{61}{4}$$
$$x = \tfrac{5}{2} \pm \tfrac{\sqrt{61}}{2}.$$

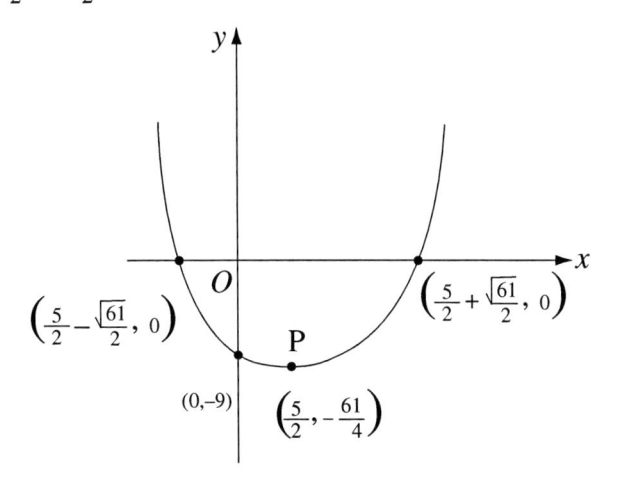

(b) $f(x) = \left(x - \tfrac{5}{2}\right)^2 - \tfrac{61}{4}$

$f\left(\tfrac{5}{2}\right) = -\tfrac{61}{4}$

$\therefore P\left(\tfrac{5}{2}, -\tfrac{61}{4}\right).$

---

4. (a)

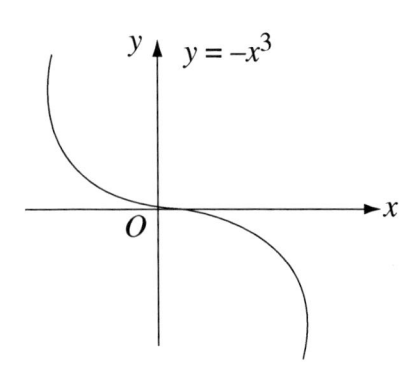

(b) (i) $f(-x) = -(-x)^3$
$= x^3$

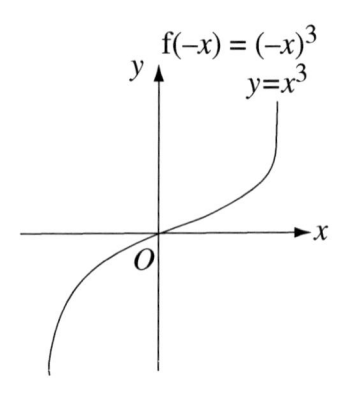

$f(-x) = (-x)^3$
$y = x^3$

(ii) $y = f(2x)$

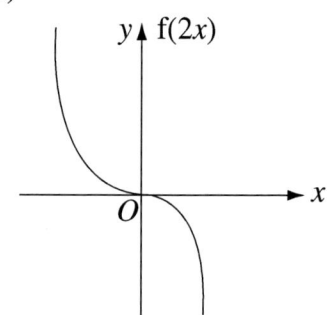

f(2x)

---

5. $f(x) = -(x+1)(x-5)$
$= -(x^2 - 4x - 5)$
$= -[(x-2)^2 - 4 - 5]$
$= -(x-2)^2 + 9$
$f(2) = 9$.

The coordinates of the maximum point are (2,9).

6. $m = \frac{5-0}{0-(-4)} = \frac{5}{4}$
   $y = \frac{5}{4}x + 5$
   $5x - 4y + 20 = 0$.

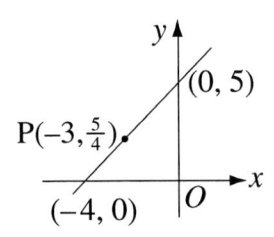

(b) if $x = -3$, $-15 - 4y + 20 = 0$
   $-4y = -5 \Rightarrow y = \frac{5}{4}$
   $\therefore P\left(-3, \frac{5}{4}\right)$ lies on the line.

(c) The gradient of the perpendicular line is $-\frac{4}{5}$, therefore $y = -\frac{4}{5}x + c$
   when $x = -3$, $y = \frac{5}{4}$

$$\frac{5}{4} = -\frac{4}{5}(-3) + c$$
$$\frac{5}{4} - \frac{12}{5} = c = \frac{25-48}{20} = -\frac{23}{20}$$
$$y = -\frac{4}{5}x - \frac{23}{20}$$
$$20y = -16x - 23$$
$$16x + 20y + 23 = 0$$
$$a = 16, \quad b = 20, \quad c = 23.$$

7. (a) $-x^2 + 2x + 3 = -(x^2 - 2x - 3)$
   $\qquad\qquad\qquad = -(x-3)(x+1) = f(x)$.

(b) $f(x) = 0$, $P(-1, 0)$, $Q(3, 0)$
   $f(0) = 3$ $\therefore R(0, 3)$.

(c) $\int_0^3 (-x^2 + 2x + 3)dx = \left[-\frac{x^3}{3} + \frac{2x^2}{2} + 3x \right]_0^3$

$= -\frac{27}{3} + 9 + 9 = 9$ s.u.

(d) $-(x^2 - 2x - 3) = -[(x-1)^2 - 1 - 3] = -(x-1)^2 + 4$

$S(1, 4)$.

---

8. (a) $f(x) = y = (x-2)(x^2 - 9) = 0$

$x = 2, \quad x = 3, \quad x = -3$

$\therefore P(-3, 0), \quad Q(2, 0), \quad R(3, 0)$.

(b) $y = (x-2)(x^2 - 9) = x^3 - 2x^2 - 9x + 18$

$\frac{dy}{dx} = 3x^2 - 4x - 9$.

(c) At $x = -2$, the gradient is given $m = 3(-2)^2 - 4(-2) - 9 = 12 + 8 - 9 = 11$

$\therefore y = mx + c$

$y = 11x + c$

$20 = 11(-2) + c$

$42 = c$

$\boxed{y = 11x + 42}$.

(d) $y = (x-2)(x^2 - 9) = x^3 - 9x - 2x^2 + 18 = x^3 - 2x^2 - 9x + 18$

$\frac{dy}{dx} = 3x^2 - 4x - 9 = 11 =$ gradient when $x = -2$

$3x^2 - 4x - 20 = 0$

$x = \frac{4 \pm \sqrt{16 + 240}}{6}$

$x = \frac{4 \pm 16}{6}$

$x = \frac{20}{6} = \frac{10}{3}$ or $x = -2$

therefore $x = \frac{10}{3}$, the x coordinate at T.

$y = \left(\frac{10}{3} - 2\right)\left(\left(\frac{10}{3}\right)^2 - 9\right)$

$ = \frac{4}{3}\left(\frac{100-81}{9}\right)$

$ = \frac{4 \times 19}{27} = \frac{76}{27}$

$T\left(\frac{10}{3}, \frac{76}{27}\right)$ the exact coordinates.

---

9. (i) Let a, b, c be the first three terms of an arithmetic progression
$b - a = c - b = d = $ common difference.

(ii) $b + b = a + c$
$2b = a + c$
$b = \frac{a+c}{2}$ the arithmetic mean.

(iii) $T_n = a + (n-1)(b-a)$
$ = a + bn - b - an + a$
$ = 2a - b + n(b-a)$.

(iv) $S_n = \frac{n}{2}[a + 2a - b + n(b-a)]$
$ = \frac{n}{2}[3a - b + n(b-a)]$.

---

10. (a) $f(x) = \frac{3}{\sqrt{x}} - \frac{5}{x^2} + \frac{7}{x^3} + 9$

$ = 3x^{-\frac{1}{2}} - 5x^{-2} + 7x^{-3} + 9$

$f'(x) = -\frac{3}{2}x^{-\frac{3}{2}} + 10x^{-3} - 21x^{-4}$

$f'(1) = -\frac{3}{2} + 10 - 21$

$ = -12\frac{1}{2} = -\frac{25}{2}$.

(b) $\frac{dy}{dx} = 3x^{\frac{1}{2}}$

$dy = 3x^{\frac{1}{2}} dx$

integrating both sides

$y = \int 3x^{\frac{1}{2}} dx = \frac{3x^{\frac{3}{2}}}{\frac{3}{2}} + c$

$y = 2x^{\frac{3}{2}} + c$ which is the general solution.

The curve passes through the point (1, 0) when $x = 1, y = 0$ substituting we have

$0 = 2(1) + c$

$c = -2$

$y = 2x^{\frac{3}{2}} - 2$

which is the particular solution.

TOTAL FOR PAPER: 75 MARKS

GCE Examinations
Advanced Subsidiary

Test Paper 5

Core Mathematics C1
Time: 1 hour 30 minutes

Instructions and Information

Candidates are not allowed to use calculators for this paper.

Full marks are awarded for answers to ALL questions.

This paper has ten questions.

You can start working with any question and you must label clearly all parts.

This paper may be reproduced in accordance with PASS PUBLICATIONS (Private Academic & Scientific Studies Limited)

1. Factorise $x^2 - 14x + 24$ by using the completing the square method and hence solve $x^2 - 14x + 24 = 0$. **(6)**

2. The general quadratic equation is given $y = ax^2 + bx + c = 0$ show that
$$x = \frac{-b \pm \sqrt{b^2 - 4ac}}{2a}.$$
(6)

3. Show algebraically that if $a > 0$ in question (2), the quadratic function has a minimum and if $a < 0$, the quadratic function has a maximum. **(8)**

4. if $x - y = 7$
   $xy = 120$. **(6)**

   Find x and y.
   Sketch the graphs and indicate the coordinates of the points of intersections. **(4)**

5. If $f(x) = 3x^{\frac{1}{3}} - \frac{1}{\sqrt[3]{x}} + x^2 - 7$,

   find (i) $f'(x)$ **(3)**

   (ii) $\int f(x)dx$. **(3)**

6. Solve $y = x^2$
   $3 \leq x^2 \leq 5$. **(4)**

7.

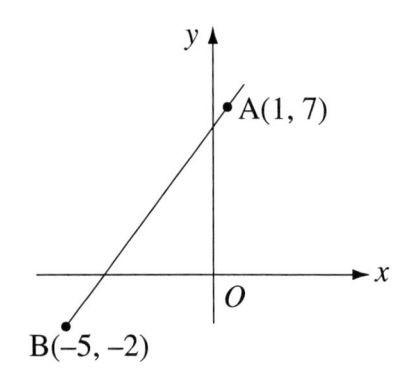

(a) Determine the gradient of AB. **(3)**

(b) Find the equation of the line in the intercept form $\frac{x}{a} + \frac{y}{b} = 1$. **(5)**

Points shown: A(1, 7), B(−5, −2).

8.

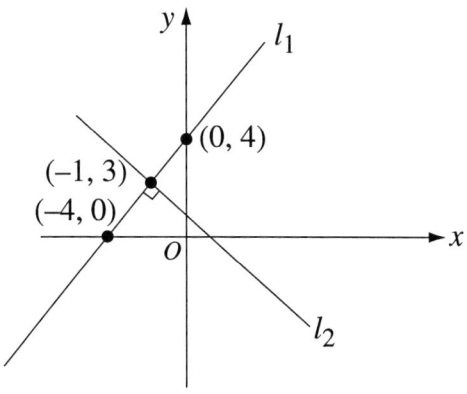

Points shown on l_1: (−4, 0), (−1, 3), (0, 4). l_2 is perpendicular to l_1 at (−1, 3).

Find the equation of l_1. l_2 is perpendicular to l_1 at the point $(-1, 3)$, find the equation of l_2. **(6)**

9. (a) The first three terms of an arithmetic progression are p, q and r. Show that $q = \frac{p+r}{2}$. **(4)**

(b) Find the nth term in terms of p and q. **(4)**

(c) Find the sum of n terms in terms of p and q. **(4)**

10.

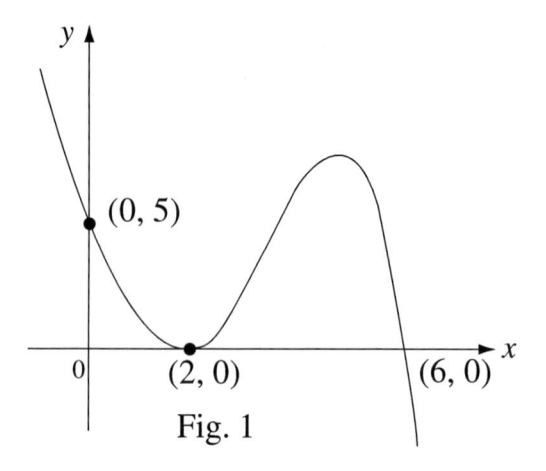

Fig. 1

Fig.1 shows a sketch of the curve with equation $y = f(x)$. The curve passes through the points (0, 5) and (6, 0) and touches the x-axis at the point (2, 0). On separate diagrams, sketch the curve with equation

(a) $y = f(x + 2)$ **(3)**

(b) $y = f(2x)$ **(3)**

(c) $y = f\left(\frac{1}{2}x\right)$. **(3)**

On each diagram show clearly the coordinates of all the points at which the curve meets the axes.

TOTAL FOR PAPER: 75 MARKS

GCE Examinations
Advanced Subsidiary

Test Paper 5 Solutions

Core Mathematics C1
Time: 1 hour 30 minutes

Instructions and Information

Candidate are not allowed to use calculators for this paper.

Full marks are awarded for answers to ALL questions.

This paper has ten questions.

You can start working with any question and you must label clearly all parts.

This paper may be reproduced in accordance with PASS PUBLICATIONS (Private Academic & Scientific Studies Limited)

1. $x^2 - 14x + 24 = (x - 7)^2 - 49 + 24$
   look at the coefficient of x, it is -14, halve it, it is -7 square it $(x - 1)^2$
   and complete it $(x - 7)^2 - 49$, that is,

$$x^2 - 14x \equiv (x - 7)^2 - 49$$
$$\equiv x^2 - 14x + 49 - 49$$
$$\equiv x^2 - 14x$$

$$\therefore x^2 - 14x + 24 = (x - 7)^2 - 25$$
$$= (x - 7)^2 - 5^2$$
$$= (x - 7 - 5)(x - 7 + 5)$$
$$= (x - 12)(x - 2)$$
$$\therefore (x - 12)(x - 2) = 0$$

$x = 2$ or $x = 12$.

---

2. $ax^2 + bx + c = a(x^2 + \frac{b}{a}x + \frac{c}{a}) = 0$
   dividing both sides by a given that $a \neq 0$

$$x^2 + \frac{b}{a}x + \frac{c}{a} = 0$$

$$\left(x + \frac{b}{2a}\right)^2 - \left(\frac{b}{2a}\right)^2 + \frac{c}{a} = 0$$

$$\left(x + \frac{b}{2a}\right)^2 = \frac{b^2}{4a^2} - \frac{c}{a} = \frac{b^2 - 4ac}{4a^2}$$

square rooting both sides

$$x + \frac{b}{2a} = \pm\frac{\sqrt{b^2 - 4ac}}{2a}$$

$$\therefore x = \frac{-b \pm \sqrt{b^2 - 4ac}}{2a}.$$

3. $f(x) = ax^2 + bx + c = a\left(x^2 + \frac{b}{a}x + \frac{c}{a}\right)$

$$f(x) = a\left[\left(x + \frac{b}{2a}\right)^2 - \frac{b^2}{4a^2} + \frac{c}{a}\right]$$

$$f(x) = a\left[\left(x + \frac{b}{2a}\right)^2 - \frac{b^2 - 4ac}{4a^2}\right]$$

$$f(x) = a\left(x + \frac{b}{2a}\right)^2 - \frac{b^2 - 4ac}{4a}$$

$$f(x) = ak - \frac{b^2 - 4ac}{4a}$$

where $k = \left(x - \frac{b}{2a}\right)^2$ is always positive since the binomial is squared.

If $a > 0$, that is, a is positive then $ak > 0$, the minimum value of the function $f(x)$, is $f(x)_{min} = -\frac{b^2 - 4ac}{4a}$, which occurs when $k = 0$, or $x = -\frac{b}{2a}$.

$f(x)_{min} = -\frac{D}{4a}$, where $D = b^2 - 4ac$ is the discriminant.

If $a < 0$, that is, a is negative, then $ak < 0$, and the maximum value of the function $f(x)$, $f(x)_{max} = -\frac{b^2 - 4ac}{4a}$, which occurs when $k = 0$, or $\left(x + \frac{b}{2a}\right)^2 = 0$, or $x = -\frac{b}{2a}$, $f(x)_{max} = -\frac{D}{4a}$ where $D = b^2 - 4ac$ is the discriminant.

---

4. $x - y = 7 \ldots (1)$
$xy = 120 \ldots (2)$
From (2) $y = \frac{120}{x} \ldots (3)$
substituting (3) in (1)

$$x - \frac{120}{x} = 7$$
$$x^2 - 120 = 7x$$
$$x^2 - 7x - 120 = 0$$
$$x^2 - 15x + 8x - 120 = 0$$
$$x(x - 15) + 8(x - 15) = 0$$
$$(x - 15)(x + 8) = 0$$
$$x = 15, \quad x = -8$$

substituting $x = 15$ in (3) we have $y = \dfrac{120}{15} = 8$
substituting $x = -8$ in (3) we have $y = -15$
$y = 8, x = -15$
$\therefore (15, 8), (-8, -15).$

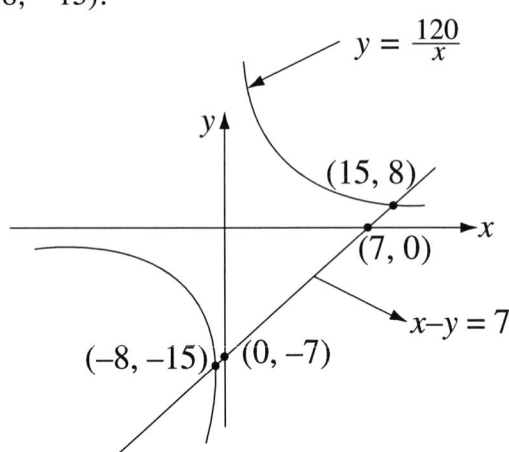

Graph showing $y = \dfrac{120}{x}$, line $x - y = 7$, with points $(15, 8)$, $(7, 0)$, $(0, -7)$, $(-8, -15)$.

5. (i) $f(x) = 3x^{\frac{1}{3}} - \dfrac{1}{\sqrt[3]{x}} + x^2 - 7 = 3x^{\frac{1}{3}} - x^{-\frac{1}{3}} + x^2 - 7.$

(ii) $f'(x) = 3\left(\dfrac{1}{3}\right)x^{-\frac{2}{3}} + \dfrac{1}{3}x^{-\frac{4}{3}} + 2x$

$= x^{-\frac{2}{3}} + \dfrac{1}{3\sqrt[3]{x^4}} + 2x.$

(iii) $\int \left(3x^{\frac{1}{3}} - x^{-\frac{1}{3}} + x^2 - 7\right) dx$

$= \dfrac{3x^{\frac{4}{3}}}{\frac{4}{3}} - \dfrac{x^{\frac{2}{3}}}{\frac{2}{3}} + \dfrac{x^3}{3} - 7x + c$

$= \dfrac{9}{4}x^{\frac{4}{3}} - \dfrac{3}{2}x^{\frac{2}{3}} + \dfrac{x^3}{3} - 7x + c.$

6.

$-\sqrt{5} \leq x \leq -\sqrt{3}$

$\sqrt{3} \leq x \leq \sqrt{5}.$

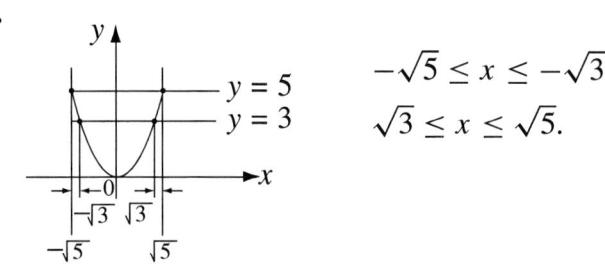

7. (a) $m = \frac{7-(-2)}{1-(-5)} = \frac{9}{6} = \frac{3}{2}.$

   (b) $y = \frac{3}{2}x + c$
   the line passes through A(1, 7)
   $7 = \frac{3}{2} + c \Rightarrow c = \frac{11}{2}$
   $y = \frac{3}{2}x + \frac{11}{2}$
   $\frac{\frac{3}{2}x}{-\frac{11}{2}} - \frac{y}{-\frac{11}{2}} = 1$
   $\frac{x}{-\frac{11}{3}} - \frac{y}{-\frac{11}{2}} = 1$
   $\frac{x}{\left(-\frac{11}{3}\right)} + \frac{y}{\left(\frac{11}{2}\right)} = 1.$

---

8. $m = \frac{4-0}{0-(-4)} = 1$
   $y = x + c$
   $\boxed{y = x + 4}$ for l_1.
   The gradient of l_2 is -1
   $y = -x + c$
   $3 = -(-1) + c$
   $c = 2$
   $\boxed{y = -x + 2.}$

---

9. (a) $q - p = d =$ common difference
   $r - q = d$
   $\therefore q - p = r - q$
   $2q = p + r$

$$q = \frac{p+r}{2}.$$

(b) $T_n = a + (n-1)d$
$T_n = p + (n-1)(q-p)$
$ = p + n(q-p) - q + p$
$T_n = 2p - q + n(q-p).$

(c) $S_n = \frac{n}{2}[a + T_n] = \frac{n}{2}[p + 2p - q + n(d-p)]$
$ = \frac{n}{2}[3p - q + n(d-p)].$

---

10. (a)

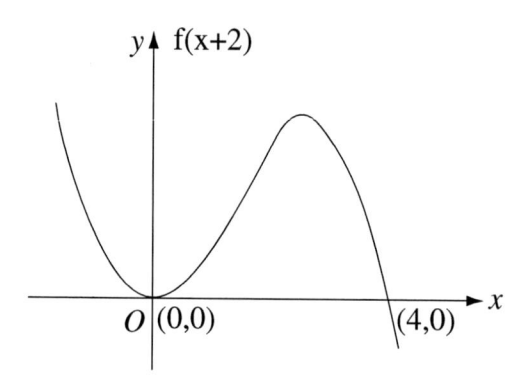

Graph of $y = f(x+2)$ passing through $O(0,0)$ and $(4,0)$.

(b)

Graph of $y = f(2x)$ passing through $(0,5)$, $(1,0)$ and $(3,0)$.

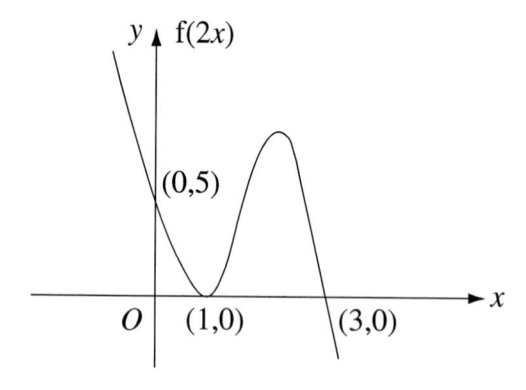

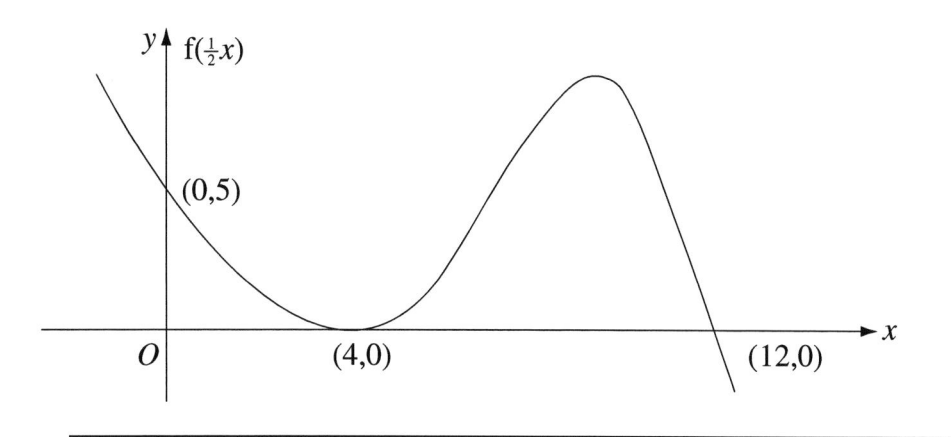

Graph of $f(\tfrac{1}{2}x)$ with points $(0,5)$, $(4,0)$, and $(12,0)$ marked.

TOTAL FOR PAPER: 75 MARKS

GCE Examinations
Advanced Subsidiary

Test Paper 6

Core Mathematics C1
Time: 1 hour 30 minutes

Instructions and Information

Candidates are not allowed to use calculators for this paper.

Full marks are awarded for answers to ALL questions.

This paper has ten questions.

You can start working with any question and you must label clearly all parts.

1. If $x^2 - kx + k - 1 = 0$, using the method of completing the square, show that the roots are

$$x = k - 1 \quad \text{or} \quad x = 1.$$ (6)

2. Explain and sketch the graphs of $ax^2 + bx + c$ when $a > 0$ for
   (i) $D = b^2 - 4ac > 0$ (2)
   (ii) $D = b^2 - 4ac = 0$ (2)
   (iii) $D < 0$. (2)

3. Find the equation of the line l_1 joining the points $A(-2, 5)$ and $B(5, -2)$. (4)
   Show that these points lie on the curve $x^2 + y^2 = 29$.
   Sketch this curve. (4)
   Find the equation of the perpendicular line l_2, passing through the origin. (4)

4. (a) $x + y = 2$ ... (1)
   $x^2 + y^2 = 10$ ... (2)
   Solve the simultaneous equations. (3)

   (b) Sketch the curves (1) and (2) and indicate the coordinates on the diagram. (10)

5. Solve $y = x^2$
   $7 \leq x^2 \leq 5$. (4)

6. (a) A curve is given by $f(x) = (x + 3)(x^2 - 25)$, show that $f'(x) = 3x^2 + 6x - 25$. (5)

   (b) Another curve is given by $g(x) = \frac{x^2 - 8x + 15}{x - 3}$ show that $g'(x) = 1$. (3)

7. Rationalise $\dfrac{1}{\sqrt{5}-\sqrt{3}}$. (2)

---

8. The nth term of the Fibonacci sequence was published in 1843 by Z. Bine, here it is

$$u_n = \dfrac{1}{\sqrt{5}}\left[\left(\dfrac{1+\sqrt{5}}{2}\right)^{n+1} - \left(\dfrac{1-\sqrt{5}}{2}\right)^{n+1}\right].$$

Find u_0, u_1, u_2 and u_3 for this sequence. (10)

---

9. An arithmetic sequence $a, a+d, a+2d, \ldots$
   (i) Deduce the nth term. (2)
   (ii) Prove that $S_n = \dfrac{n}{2}[2a + (n-1)d] = \dfrac{n}{2}[a + T_n]$ where $T_n = a + (n-1)d$. (8)

10.

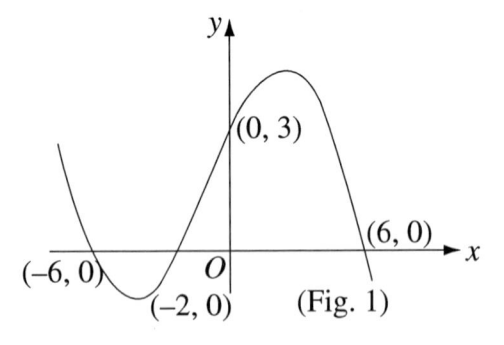

(Fig. 1)

Fig. 1 shows a sketch of the curve with equation $y = f(x)$. The curve passes through the points $(-6, 0), (-2, 0), (0, 3)$ and $(6, 0)$.
On separate diagrams sketch the curve with equation

(a) $y = f(x-4)$ (2)

(b) $y = 2f(x)$ (2)

(c) $y = f(2x)$. (2)

On each diagram show clearly the coordinates of all the points at which the curve meets the axes.

TOTAL FOR PAPER: 75 MARKS

GCE Examinations
Advanced Subsidiary

Test Paper 6 Solutions

Core Mathematics C1
Time: 1 hour 30 minutes

Instructions and Information

Candidates are not allowed to use calculators for this paper.

Full marks are awarded for answers to ALL questions.

This paper has ten questions.

You can start working with any question and you must label clearly all parts.

1. $x^2 - kx + k - 1 = 0$
$\left(x - \frac{k}{2}\right)^2 - \left(-\frac{k}{2}\right)^2 + k - 1 = 0$
$\left(x - \frac{k}{2}\right)^2 = \frac{k^2}{4} - k + 1 = \frac{k^2 - 4k + 4}{4}$
$\left(x - \frac{k}{2}\right)^2 = \frac{(k-2)^2}{4}$
square rooting both sides
$x - \frac{k}{2} = \pm \frac{(k-2)}{2}$
$x = \frac{k \pm (k-2)}{2}$
$x = \frac{2k-2}{2} = k - 1$
$x = \frac{k-k+2}{2} = 1$.

---

2. (i)

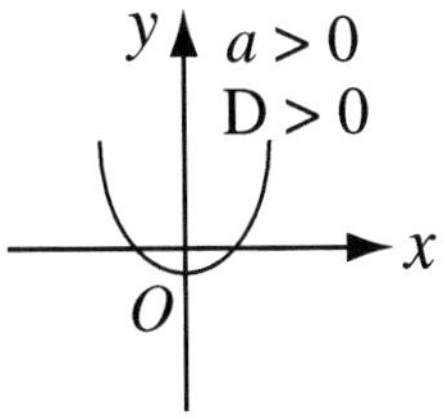

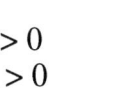

y, $a > 0$, $D > 0$

(ii)

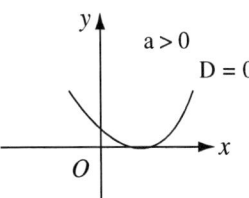

y, $a > 0$, $D = 0$

(iii)

y, $a > 0$, $D < 0$

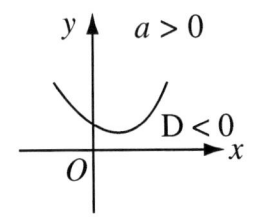

$a > 0$, indicates that the curve has a minimum
$D < 0$ indicates that the curve neither intersects nor touches the x-axis, there are no real roots, the roots are complex.

3.

The gradient $= m = \frac{5-(-2)}{-2-5}$

$= \frac{7}{-7} = -1$

$y = mx + c$

$5 = -(-2) + c$

$\boxed{y = -x + 3}$

Check that the points $(-2, 5)$ and $(5, -2)$ lie on the curve
$(-2)^2 + (5)^2 = (5)^2 + (-2)^2 = 29$.
The gradient of the line through the origin is 1
$\therefore y = x + c$, since $a = 0, y = 0$
$\boxed{y = x}$.

(Diagram: y-axis, $y = x$, A(-2,5), $x^2 + y^2 = 29$, B(5,-2), $y = -x+3$)

---

4. (a) $x + y = 2$ ... (1)

$x^2 + y^2 = 10$ ... (2)

From (1) $y = 2 - x$ ... (3)

Substitute (3) in (2)

$$x^2 + (2 - x)^2 = 10$$

$x^2 + 4 - 4x + x^2 - 10 = 0$

$2x^2 - 4x - 6 = 0$

$x^2 - 2x - 3 = 0$

$(x - 3)(x + 1) = 0$

$x = -1, \quad x = 3$

substituting in (3)

$y = 2 - (-1) = 3$ when $x = -1$

$y = 2 - 3 = -1$ when $x = 3$

$\therefore (-1, 3), \quad (3, -1)$.

(b)

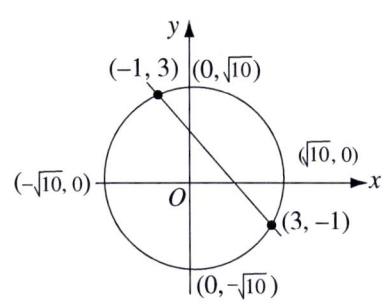

when $y = 0$, $x = \pm\sqrt{10}$
when $x = 0$, $y = \pm\sqrt{10}$.

5.

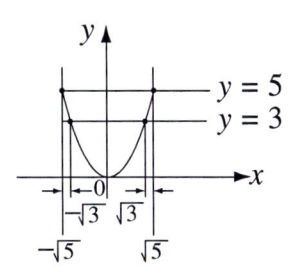

$-\sqrt{7} \le x \le -\sqrt{5}$
$\sqrt{5} \le x \le \sqrt{7}$.

6. (a) $f(x) = (x+3)(x^2 - 25)$
$= x^3 + 3x^2 - 25x - 75$
$f'(x) = 3x^2 + 6x - 25$.

(b) $g(x) = \frac{x^2-8x+15}{x-3} = \frac{(x-3)(x-5)}{x-3} = x - 5$
$g'(x) = 1$.

7. $\frac{1}{\sqrt{5}-\sqrt{3}} = \frac{\sqrt{5}+\sqrt{3}}{(\sqrt{5}-\sqrt{3})(\sqrt{5}+\sqrt{3})} = \frac{\sqrt{5}+\sqrt{3}}{5-3}$
$= \frac{1}{2}\sqrt{5} + \frac{1}{2}\sqrt{3}$.

8. $u_n = \frac{1}{\sqrt{5}}\left[\left(\frac{1+\sqrt{5}}{2}\right)^{n+1} - \left(\frac{1-\sqrt{5}}{2}\right)^{n+1}\right]$

$u_0 = \frac{1}{\sqrt{5}}\left(\frac{1+\sqrt{5}}{2} - \frac{1-\sqrt{5}}{2}\right) = 1$

$u_1 = \frac{1}{\sqrt{5}}\left[\left(\frac{1+\sqrt{5}}{2}\right)^2 - \left(\frac{1-\sqrt{5}}{2}\right)^2\right]$

$ = \frac{1}{\sqrt{5}}\left(\frac{1+2\sqrt{5}+5}{4} - \frac{1-2\sqrt{5}+5}{4}\right)$

$ = \frac{1}{\sqrt{5}}\left(\frac{6}{4} + \frac{\sqrt{5}}{2} - \frac{6}{4} + \frac{\sqrt{5}}{2}\right) = 1$

$u_2 = \frac{1}{\sqrt{5}}\left[\left(\frac{1+\sqrt{5}}{2}\right)^3 - \left(\frac{1-\sqrt{5}}{2}\right)^3\right]$

$ = \frac{1}{\sqrt{5}}\left(\frac{1+3\sqrt{5}+15+5\sqrt{5}}{8} - \frac{1-3\sqrt{5}+15-5\sqrt{5}}{8}\right)$

$ = \frac{1}{\sqrt{5}}\frac{(16\sqrt{5})}{8}) = 2$

$u_3 = \frac{1}{\sqrt{5}}\left[\left(\frac{1+\sqrt{5}}{2}\right)^4 - \left(\frac{1-\sqrt{5}}{2}\right)^4\right]$

$ = \frac{1}{\sqrt{5}}\left[\frac{(1+2\sqrt{5}+5)^2}{16} - \frac{(1-2\sqrt{5}+5)^2}{16}\right]$

$ = \frac{1}{\sqrt{5}}\left[\frac{(6+2\sqrt{5})^2}{16} - \frac{(6-2\sqrt{5})^2}{16}\right]$

$ = \frac{1}{16\sqrt{5}}\left[6+2\sqrt{5} - (6-2\sqrt{5})\right]\left[6+2\sqrt{5}+6-2\sqrt{5}\right]$

$ = \frac{1}{16\sqrt{5}}\left(4\sqrt{5}\right)(12)$

$ = \frac{48\sqrt{5}}{16\sqrt{5}} = 3$

u_0, u_1, u_2, u_3

1, 1, 2, 3.

9. $a, a+d, a+2d, a+3d, \ldots a+(n-1)d$
$1^{st} \quad 2^{nd} \quad 3^{rd} \quad 4^{th} \qquad n^{th}$
$T_n = a + (n-1)d$
$S_n = a + (a+d) + (a+2d) + \ldots + [a+(n-1)d] \ldots (1)$
$S_n = [a+(n-1)d] + [a+(n-2)d] + \ldots \qquad + a \ldots (2)$
Adding (1) and 2
$2S_n = [2a+(n-1)d] + [2a+(n-1)d] + \ldots [2a+(n-1)d]$
$2S_n = n[2a+(n-1)d]$
$2S_n = n[a+a+(n-1)d]$
$2S_n = n(a+T_n)$
$\therefore S_n = \frac{n}{2}[2a+(n-1)d] = \frac{n}{2}[a+T_n]$.

---

10. (a)

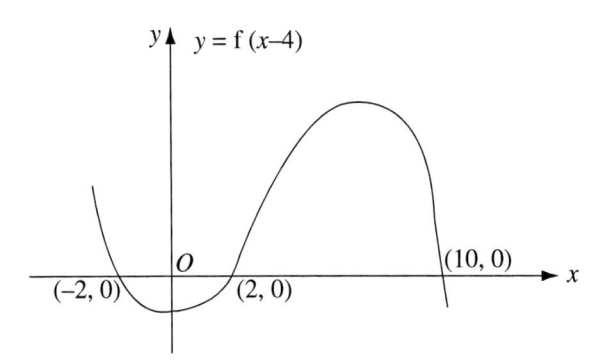

$y = f(x-4)$, points $(-2, 0)$, $(2, 0)$, $(10, 0)$

(b)

$y = 2f(x)$, points $(-6, 0)$, $(-2, 0)$, $(0, 6)$, $(6, 0)$

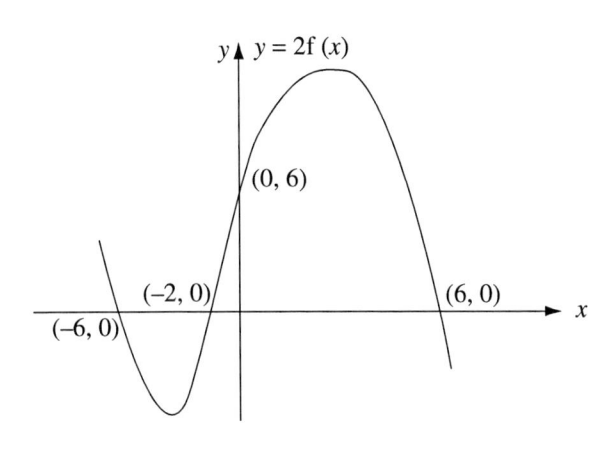

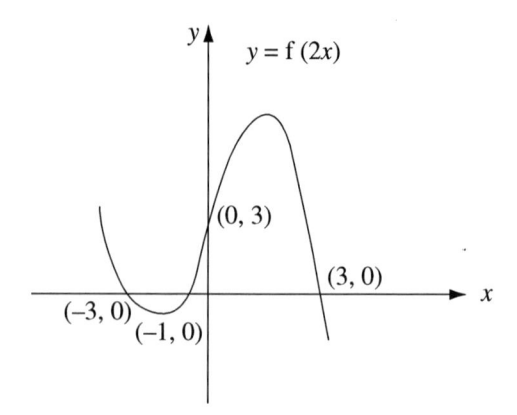

(c)

$y = f(2x)$

Points marked on graph: $(0, 3)$, $(-3, 0)$, $(-1, 0)$, $(3, 0)$

TOTAL FOR PAPER: 75 MARKS

GCE Examinations
Advanced Subsidiary

Test Paper 7

Core Mathematics C1
Time: 1 hour 30 minutes

Instructions and Information

Candidates are not allowed to use calculators for this paper.

Full marks are awarded for answers to ALL questions.

This paper has ten questions.

You can start working with any question and you must label clearly all parts.

1. (a) Evaluate $\left(12\frac{24}{25}\right)^{-\frac{1}{2}}$. (3)

   (b) Express $\frac{1}{\sqrt{6}-\sqrt{3}}$ in the form $\frac{\sqrt{3}}{a}(\sqrt{2}+b)$ where a and b are rational numbers. (4)

---

2. Solve
   (a) $x^2 - 25x + 24 = 0$, by sight (2)
   (b) $x^2 + 14x + 24 = 0$, by formula (3)
   (c) $x^2 - 11x + 24 = 0$, by completing the square method. (5)

---

3. Solve the simultaneous equations
$$x^2 + y^2 = 25 \ldots (1)$$
$$2x - y = 5 \ldots (2)$$
(4)

---

4. (a) Solve $3x - 5 > 5x + 7$. (2)
   (b) Find the set of values of x which satisfy the inequality
   $$x^2 + 4x - 12 < 0$$
   (3)

---

5. (a) Factorise $f(x) = x^3 - 3x^2 + 2x$. (2)
   (b) Sketch $y = (x - 1)^3$. (2)
   (c) Sketch $y = \frac{1}{x}$ and state the equations of the asymptotes. (3)

---

6. (a) $f(x) = \frac{1}{x-1}$, sketch $f(x - 1)$. (3)
   (b) $g(x) = (x + 1)^3$, sketch $g(x + 1)$. (3)

7. (a) Determine the equation of the straight line l_1, which passes through the two points $A(-2, 3)$ and $B(2, -3)$ in the general form $ax + by + c = 0$. (3)

(b) A perpendicular line, l_2, to l_1 passes through $(-3, -5)$, find the equation of l_2 in the form $y = mx + c$. (3)

---

8. (a) $u_{n+1} = 2u_n + 1$
if $u_0 = 1$, find u_1, u_2, u_3. (2)

(b) Find the nth term of the arithmetic sequence:
$-3, -5, -7, -9 \ldots$ (2)

(c) Find the sum of 20 terms. (2)

---

9. (a) If $f(x) = (3x - 1)(x + 4)$ find $f'(x)$, $f'(-2)$. (3)

(b) $\int f(x) dx$. (3)

---

10. (a) Sketch the graph $f(x) = (x + 2)^3$ and find $f'(x)$. (6)

(b) Find the equation of the tangent at the point $P(-4, -8)$. (4)

(c) Find the equation of the normal at the point $Q(0, 8)$. (4)

(d) Find the exact coordinates of the point of intersection of the tangent at P and the normal at Q. (4)

TOTAL FOR PAPER: 75 MARKS

GCE Examinations
Advanced Subsidiary

Test Paper 7 Solutions

Core Mathematics C1
Time: 1 hour 30 minutes

Instructions and Information

Candidates are not allowed to use calculators for this paper.

Full marks are awarded for answers to ALL questions.

This paper has ten questions.

You can start working with any question and you must label clearly all parts.

1. (a) $\left(12\frac{24}{25}\right)^{-\frac{1}{2}} = \left(\frac{324}{25}\right)^{-\frac{1}{2}} = \left(\frac{25}{324}\right)^{\frac{1}{2}} = \frac{5}{18}$.

(b) $\frac{1}{\sqrt{6}-\sqrt{3}} = \frac{1}{\sqrt{6}-\sqrt{3}} \times \frac{\sqrt{6}+\sqrt{3}}{\sqrt{6}+\sqrt{3}} = \frac{\sqrt{6}+\sqrt{3}}{6-3}$

$= \frac{1}{3}\sqrt{6} + \frac{1}{3}\sqrt{3} = \frac{\sqrt{3}}{3}(\sqrt{2}+1)$

$a = 3, \quad b = 1$.

---

2. (a) $x^2 - 25x + 24 = (x-1)(x-24) = 0$

$x = 1 \text{ or } x = 24$

(b) $x^2 + 14x + 24 = 0$

$x = \frac{-14 \pm \sqrt{14^2 - 4 \times 1 \times 24}}{2 \times 1} = \frac{-14 \pm \sqrt{196-96}}{2}$

$x = \frac{-14 \pm 10}{2} \Rightarrow x = -2 \text{ or } x = -12$

(c) $x^2 - 11x + 24 = \left(x - \frac{11}{2}\right)^2 - \left(-\frac{11}{2}\right)^2 + 24$

$= \left(x - \frac{11}{2}\right)^2 - \frac{121}{4} + \frac{96}{4}$

$= \left(x - \frac{11}{2}\right)^2 - \frac{25}{4}$

$= \left[\left(x - \frac{11}{2}\right) - \frac{5}{2}\right]\left[x - \frac{11}{2} + \frac{5}{2}\right]$

$= \left(x - \frac{16}{2}\right)\left(x - \frac{6}{2}\right)$

$= (x-8)(x-3) = 0$

$x = 8 \text{ or } x = 3$.

---

3. From (2) $y = 2x - 5$

and substituting in (1) we have

$x^2 + y^2 = x^2 + (2x-5)^2$

$= x^2 + 4x^2 - 20x + 25$

$= 5x^2 - 20x + 25 = 25$

$5x^2 - 20x = 0$

$5x(x-4) = 0$

$x = 0, \quad x = 4$

$y = -5, \quad y = 3$

$\therefore (0, -5), \quad (4, 3)$.

4. (a) $3x - 5 > 5x + 7$
$-5 - 7 > 5x - 3x$
$-12 > 2x$
$2x < -12$
$\boxed{x < -6}$

(b) $x^2 + 4x - 12 < 0$
$(x + 6)(x - 2) < 0$
$\therefore -6 < x < 2.$

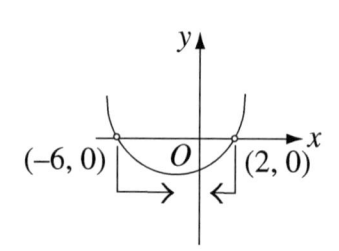

---

5. (a) $f(x) = x^3 - 3x^2 + 2x = x(x^2 - 3x + 2) = x(x - 1)(x - 2).$ (2)

(b) $y = (x - 1)^3$

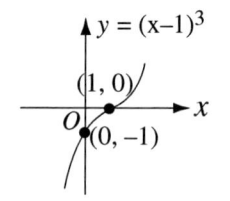

(2)

(c)

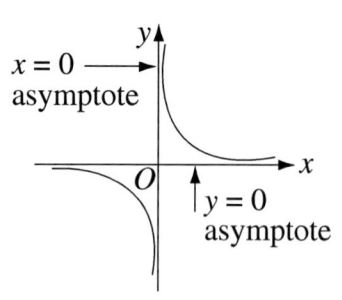

6. (a)

y = f(x−1)

x = 2

(b)

g(x+1)

(−2, 0)

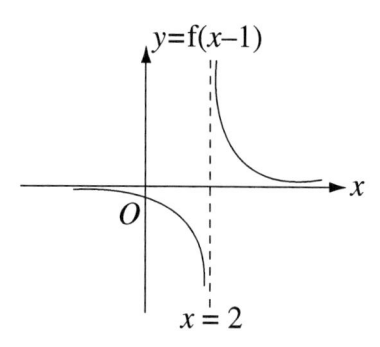

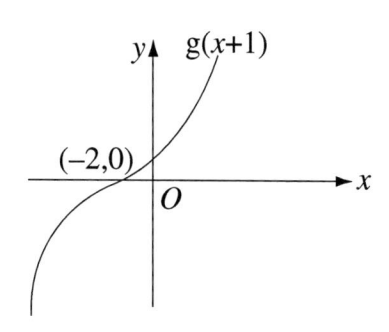

7. (a)

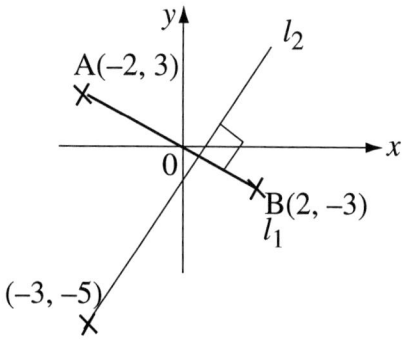

A(−2, 3)

B(2, −3), l_1

l_2

(−3, −5)

$m = \frac{3-(-3)}{-2-(2)} = -\frac{6}{4} = -\frac{3}{2}$
$y = mx + c$
$y = -\frac{3}{2}x + c$
$3 = -\frac{3}{2}(-2) + c$

$3 = 3 + c$
$c = 0$
$y = -\frac{3}{2}x$
$2y = -3x$
$$\boxed{3x + 2y = 0}$$
Equation of l_2
$y = \frac{2}{3}x + c$
$-5 = \frac{2}{3}(-3) + c \Rightarrow -5 = -2 + c$
$c = -3$
$$\boxed{y = \frac{2}{3}x - 3}.$$

---

8. (a) $u_{n+1} = 2u_n + 1$
$u_0 = 1$
$u_1 = 2u_0 + 1 = 2 \times 1 + 1 = 3$
$u_2 = 2u_1 + 1 = 2 \times 3 + 1 = 7$
$u_3 = 2u_2 + 1 = 2 \times 7 + 1 = 15$

(b) $a = -3, d = -5 - (-3) = -2$
$T_n = -3 + (n - 1)(-2) = -3 + -2n + 2$
$T_n = -1 - 2n$

(c) $S_{20} = \frac{20}{2}[2 \times (-3) + (20 - 1)(-2)]$
$= 10(-6 - 38)$
$= -440.$

---

9. (a) $f(x) = (3x - 1)(x + 4)$
$= 3x^2 - x + 12x - 4$
$= 3x^2 + 11x - 4$
$f'(x) = 6x + 11$
$f'(-2) = -12 + 11 = -1$

(b) $\int (3x^2 + 11x - 4)dx = \frac{3x^3}{3} + \frac{11x^2}{2} - 4x + c$
$= x^3 + \frac{11x^2}{2} - 4x + c.$

10. (a) $f(x) = (x+2)^3$
$f'(x) = 3(x+2)^2$
alternatively
$f(x) = x^3 + 6x^2 + 12x + 8$
$f'(x) = 3x^2 + 12x + 12$
$\qquad = 3(x^2 + 4x + 4)$
$\qquad = 3(x+2)^2.$

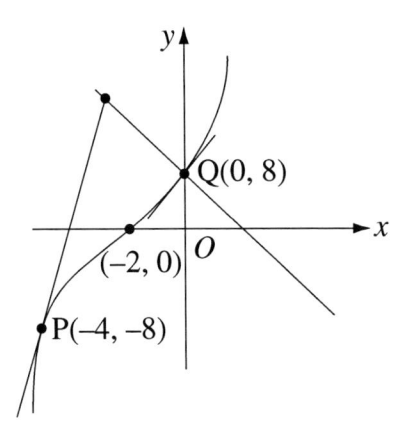

(b) At $x = -4$, $f'(-4) = 3(-4+2)^2 = 12$
$f'(-4) = 12$ the gradient at $x = -4$
$y = 12x + c$
$-8 = 12(-4) + c$
$c = -8 + 48 = 40$
$\boxed{y = 12x + 40}$ ... (1) The equation of the tangent at P.

(c) The gradient at $x = 0$ is 12, the gradient of the tangent, the gradient of the normal at Q is $-\frac{1}{12}$.

$y = -\frac{1}{12}x + c$

$8 = 0 + c \Rightarrow c = 8$

$\boxed{y = -\frac{1}{12}x + 8} \ldots (2)$

The equation of normal at Q.

$y = 12x + 40 \ldots (1)$

$y = -\frac{1}{12}x + 8 \ldots (2)$

$12x + 40 = -\frac{1}{12}x + 8$

$12x + \frac{1}{12}x = -40 + 8$

$\frac{145}{12}x = -32 \Rightarrow x = -\frac{32 \times 12}{145} = -\frac{384}{145}$

Substituting in (2)

$y = -\frac{1}{12} \times -\frac{32 \times 12}{145} + 8$

$y = \frac{32}{145} + 8 = \frac{32 + 8 \times 145}{145}$

$y = \frac{32 + 1160}{145} = \frac{1192}{145}$

$\left(-\frac{384}{145}, \frac{1192}{145}\right).$

TOTAL FOR PAPER: 75 MARKS

GCE Examinations
Advanced Subsidiary

Test Paper 8

Core Mathematics C1
Time: 1 hour 30 minutes

Instructions and Information

Candidates are not allowed to use calculators for this paper.

Full marks are awarded for answers to ALL questions.

This paper has ten questions.

You can start working with any question and you must label clearly all parts.

This paper may be reproduced in accordance with PASS PUBLICATIONS (Private Academic & Scientific Studies Limited)

1. (a) Express the indicial form $a^{\frac{m}{n}}$ to the root form. **(1 mark)**

   (b) $\left(2\frac{10}{27}\right)^{-\frac{2}{3}} = \frac{N}{D}$, find N and D which are integers. **(3 marks)**

   (c) Rationalise the denominator
   $$\frac{\sqrt{3} - \sqrt{2}}{\sqrt{3} + \sqrt{2}}.$$ **(4 marks)**

2. (a) Factorise $f(x) = 2x^2 + 9x - 5$, hence solve $f(x) = 0$. **(2 marks)**

   (b) Solve $f(x) = 0$, using the quadratic formula. **(2 marks)**

   (c) Factorise $f(x)$ by means, of the completing the square method, hence solve $f(x) = 0$. **(4 marks)**

3. Sketch the graphs

   (a) $x^2 + y^2 = 36$ ...(1)

   (b) $x + y = 6$ ...(2)

   Solve simultaneously the equations (1) and (2). **(4 marks)**

4. Fig. 1 shows a sketch of the curve with equation $y = f(x)$. The curve passes through the points $(-1, 0)$, $(0, 2)$ and $(2, 0)$. The maximum point of the curve is $(\frac{1}{2}, \frac{9}{2})$.

   On separate diagrams, sketch the curve with equations:

   (a) $y = 2f(x)$ **(2 marks)**

   (b) $y = f(x - 2)$. **(3 marks)**

On each diagram, indicate clearly the coordinates of the maximum point and the points of the intersections of the curve with the x-axis.

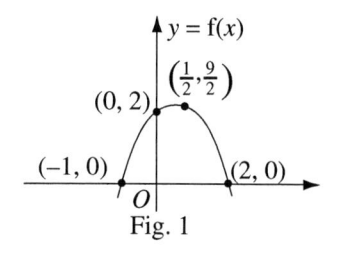

$y = f(x)$, $\left(\frac{1}{2}, \frac{9}{2}\right)$, $(0, 2)$, $(-1, 0)$, $(2, 0)$

Fig. 1

---

5. Find the set of values of x for which

(a) $5(3x - 1) > 10 + 16x$ …(1) **(2 marks)**

(b) $x^2 - 4x - 45 > 0$ …(2) **(2 marks)**

(c) both (1) and (2). **(2 marks)**

---

6. Show that $\dfrac{(5 - 2\sqrt{x})^2}{\sqrt{x}}$ can be written as $25x^{-\frac{1}{2}} - 20 + 4x^{\frac{1}{2}}$. **(2 marks)**

Given that $\dfrac{dy}{dx} = \dfrac{(5 - 2\sqrt{x})^2}{\sqrt{x}}$, $x > 0$, and that $y = 20$ at $x = 1$,

(b) find y in terms of x. **(4 marks)**

---

7. An arithmetic series has a as the first term and common difference $d = -10$.

The sum of 50 terms is given as 10000.

Determine the first term and the 50th term. **(6 marks)**

8. (a) Solve the cubic equation

   $f(x) = (x-1)(x-3)(x-5) = 0$. **(3 marks)**

   (b) Sketch the cubic function $f(x)$, justifying the shape by finding $f(1)$, $f(3)$, $f(5)$ and $f(2)$. **(3 marks)**

---

9. Given that $y = 3x^2 - \dfrac{1}{x^2}$ find the following:

   (a) $\dfrac{dy}{dx}$ **(3 marks)**

   (b) $\dfrac{d^2y}{dx^2}$ **(3 marks)**

   (c) $\int y\,dx$ **(3 marks)**

   expressing the results as positive indices.

---

10. Fig. 2 shows part of the curve with equation $y = f(x)$ where $f(x) = x^3 - 10x^2 + 21x$.

    The curve crosses the x-axis at the origin O and at the points P and Q.

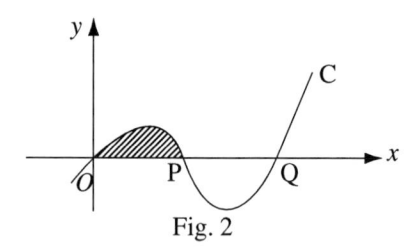

    Fig. 2

    (a) Factorise $f(x)$ completely. **(3 marks)**

    (b) Write down the x-coordinates of the points O, P and Q. **(2 marks)**

    (c) Find the exact area hatched **(6 marks)**

    (d) Find the gradients of C at O, P and Q. **(6 marks)**

TOTAL FOR PAPER: 75 MARKS

GCE Examinations
Advanced Subsidiary

Test Paper 8 Solutions

Core Mathematics C1
Time: 1 hour 30 minutes

Instructions and Information

Candidates are not allowed to use calculators for this paper.

Full marks are awarded for answers to ALL questions.

This paper has ten questions.

You can start working with any question and you must label clearly all parts.

1. (a) $a^{\frac{m}{n}} = \sqrt[n]{a^m}$.

   (b) $\left(2\dfrac{10}{27}\right)^{-\frac{2}{3}} = \left(\dfrac{64}{27}\right)^{-\frac{2}{3}} = \left(\dfrac{27}{64}\right)^{\frac{2}{3}} = \left(\dfrac{3}{4}\right)^2$

   $= \dfrac{9}{16}.$

   (c) $\dfrac{\sqrt{3}-\sqrt{2}}{\sqrt{3}+\sqrt{2}} = \dfrac{\left(\sqrt{3}-\sqrt{2}\right)}{\sqrt{3}+\sqrt{2}} \times \dfrac{\left(\sqrt{3}-\sqrt{2}\right)}{\sqrt{3}-\sqrt{2}}$

   $= \dfrac{\left(\sqrt{3}-\sqrt{2}\right)^2}{(\sqrt{3})^2 - (\sqrt{2})^2} = \dfrac{3 - 2\sqrt{3}\sqrt{2} + 2}{3 - 2}$

   $= 5 - 2\sqrt{6}.$

---

2. (a) $2x^2 + 9x - 5 = (2x-1)(x+5) = 0$

   $x = -5 \text{ or } x = \dfrac{1}{2}.$

   (b) $x = \dfrac{-9 \pm \sqrt{81 - 4(2)(-5)}}{8 \times 2} = \dfrac{-9 \pm \sqrt{121}}{4}$

   $= -\dfrac{9}{4} \pm \dfrac{11}{4}$

   $\therefore x = -\dfrac{9}{4} + \dfrac{11}{4} = \dfrac{1}{2} \text{ or } x = -\dfrac{20}{4} = -5.$

   (c) $2x^2 + 9x - 5 = 2\left(x^2 + \dfrac{9}{2}x - \dfrac{5}{2}\right)$

   $= 2\left[\left(x + \dfrac{9}{4}\right)^2 - \left(\dfrac{9}{4}\right)^2 - \dfrac{5}{2}\right]$

$$= 2\left[\left(x+\frac{9}{4}\right)^2 - \frac{81}{16} - \frac{40}{16}\right] = 2\left[\left(x+\frac{9}{4}\right)^2 - \frac{121}{16}\right]$$

$$= 2\left[\left(x+\frac{9}{4}\right)^2 - \left(\frac{11}{4}\right)^2\right]$$

$$= 2\left(x+\frac{9}{4}-\frac{11}{4}\right)\left(x+\frac{9}{4}+\frac{11}{4}\right)$$

$$= 2\left(x-\frac{1}{2}\right)(x+5) = (2x-1)(x+5) = 0$$

$$x = \frac{1}{2} \text{ or } x = -5.$$

---

3. $x^2 + y = 36$ ...(1)

   $x + y = 6$ ...(2)

   From (2)

   $y = 6 - x$

   substituting in (1)

   $x^2 + (6-x)^2 = 36$

   $x^2 + 36 - 12x + x^2 - 36 = 0$

   $2x^2 - 12x = 0$

   $2x(x-6) = 0$

   $x = 0, x = 6$

   $y = 6, y = 0$

$A(0, 6)$ and $B(6, 0)$.

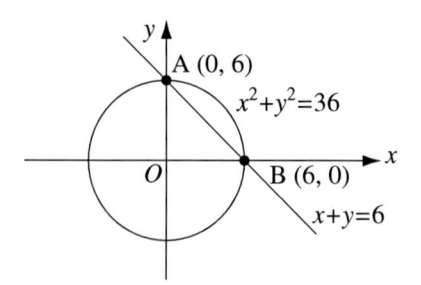

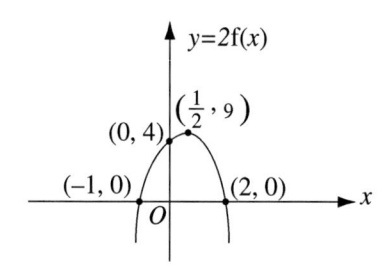

(diagram: circle $x^2+y^2=36$ with line $x+y=6$ passing through $A(0,6)$ and $B(6,0)$)

4. (a)

(diagram: graph of $y=2f(x)$, downward parabola through $(-1,0)$, $(0,4)$, $(2,0)$ with maximum at $(\frac{1}{2}, 9)$)

(b)

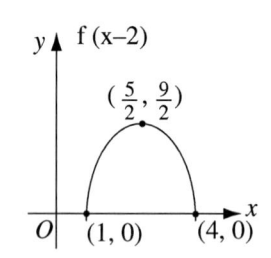

(diagram: graph of $f(x-2)$, through $(1,0)$, $(4,0)$ with maximum at $(\frac{5}{2}, \frac{9}{2})$)

5. (a) $5(3x - 1) > 10 + 16x$

$15x - 5 > 10 + 16x$

$15x - 16x > 10 + 5$

$-x > 15$

$$x < -15$$

(b) $x^2 - 4x - 45 > 0$

$(x-9)(x+5) > 0$

$x < -5, x > 9$

(c) $x < -15$.

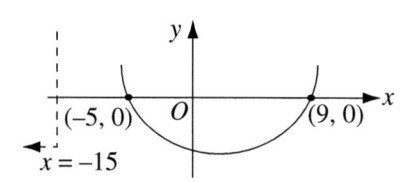

---

6. (a) $\dfrac{(5-2\sqrt{x})^2}{\sqrt{x}} = \dfrac{25 - 20\sqrt{x} + 4x}{\sqrt{x}} = \dfrac{25 - 20x^{\frac{1}{2}} + 4x}{x^{\frac{1}{2}}}$

$= 25x^{-\frac{1}{2}} - 20 + 4x^{\frac{1}{2}}$.

(b) $\dfrac{dy}{dx} = \dfrac{(5-2\sqrt{x})^2}{\sqrt{x}} = 25x^{-\frac{1}{2}} - 20 + 4x^{\frac{1}{2}}$

$dy = \left(25x^{-\frac{1}{2}} - 20 + 4x^{\frac{1}{2}}\right) dx$

$\int dy = \int \left(25x^{-\frac{1}{2}} - 20 + 4x^{\frac{1}{2}}\right) dx$

$y = \dfrac{25x^{\frac{1}{2}}}{\frac{1}{2}} - 20x + \dfrac{4x^{\frac{3}{2}}}{\frac{3}{2}} + c$

$y = 50x^{\frac{1}{2}} - 20x + \dfrac{8}{3}x^{\frac{3}{2}} + c$

$20 = 50 \times 1 - 20 + \dfrac{8}{3} + c$

$20 - 32\frac{2}{3} = c$

$c = -12\frac{2}{3}$

$$\therefore y = 50\sqrt{x} - 20x + \tfrac{8}{3}x^{\frac{3}{2}} - 12\tfrac{2}{3}.$$

7. $S_{50} = \dfrac{50}{2}[2a + (50-1)(-10)] = 10000$
$= 50[a + 49(-5)] = 10000$
$a - 5 \times 49 = 200$
$a = 200 + 245$
$a = 445.$
The 50th term is $T_{50} = 445 + (50-1)(-10)$
$= 445 - 490$
$= -45.$

8. (a) $f(x) = (x-1)(x-3)(x-5) = 0$
$x - 1 = 0 \Rightarrow x = 1$
or $x - 3 = 0 \Rightarrow x = 3$
or $x - 5 = 0 \Rightarrow x = 5.$

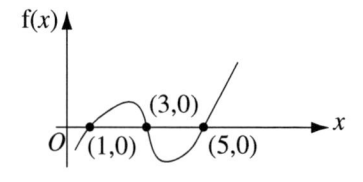

(b) $f(0) = (-1)(-3)(-5) = -15$
$f(1) = (0), f(3) = 0, f(5) = 0$
$f(2) = (2-1)(2-3)(2-5) = 1 \times (-1)(-3) = 3.$

9. (a) $y = 3x^2 - \dfrac{1}{x^2} = 3x^2 - x^{-2}$

$$\frac{dy}{dx} = 6x + 2x^{-3} = 6x + \frac{2}{x^3}$$

(b) $\frac{d^2y}{dx} = 6 - 6x^{-4} = 6 - \frac{6}{x^4}$

(c) $\int y\,dx = \int(3x^2 - x^{-2})dx = \frac{3x^3}{3} - \frac{x^{-1}}{-1} + c$

$\quad\quad\quad = x^3 + \frac{1}{x} + c.$

---

10. (a) $f(x) = x^3 - 10x^2 + 21x$

$\quad\quad = x(x^2 - 10x + 21)$

$\quad\quad = x(x-3)(x-7).$

(b) $O(0,0)$, $P(3,0)$, $Q(7,0).$

(c) $\int_0^3 (x^3 - 10x^2 + 21x)dx$

$\left[\frac{x^4}{4} - \frac{10x^3}{3} + \frac{21x^2}{2}\right]_0^3$

$\quad = \frac{81}{4} - \frac{10}{3}(27) + \frac{21(9)}{2} = \frac{81}{4} - \frac{270}{3} + \frac{189}{2}$

$\quad = \frac{3 \times 81 - 270 \times 4 + 189 \times 6}{12}$

$\quad = \frac{243 - 1080 + 1134}{12} = \frac{297}{12} = 24\frac{3}{4}.$

(d) $f'(x) = 3x^2 - 20x + 21$

$f'(0) = 21$

$f'(3) = 3 \times 9 - 20 \times 3 + 21 = 27 - 60 + 21$

$\quad = -12$

$f'(7) = 3 \times 7^2 - 20x7 + 21$

$\quad = 3 \times 49 - 140 + 21$

$\quad = 147 - 140 + 21$

$\quad = 28.$

GCE Examinations
Advanced Subsidiary

Test Paper 9

Core Mathematics C1
Time: 1 hour 30 minutes

Instructions and Information

Candidates are not allowed to use calculators for this paper.

Full marks are awarded for answers to ALL questions.

This paper has ten questions.

You can start working with any question and you must label clearly all parts.

1. The nth term of a positive sequence is given $u_n = 2 + 3^n$.

   (a) Write down the first five terms of the sequence. (3)

   (b) Evaluate $\sum_{n=1}^{5} u_n$. (3)

   (c) Show that the sequence is not arithmetic. (2)

   (d) Find an expression of $u_{n+1} - u_n$. (3)

---

2. Simplify $\frac{5}{\sqrt{50}}$ with rational denominator. (2)

---

3. (a) Solve the inequality $x^2(x - 1) > 0$. (2)

   (b) Solve the inequality $x(x - 1) > 0$. (3)

---

4. (a) Find a, when $a^6 = 64 \times 16^3$. (3)

   (b) Find b, when $b = \left(\frac{32}{243}\right)^{-\frac{2}{5}}$ and it is rational. (3)

---

5. Calculate (a) $\int \frac{3x^3}{4} dx$ (b) $\int \frac{x^2-1}{x+1} dx$. (5)

---

6. Solve the quadratic equation,

$$x^2 + 25x + 24 = 0$$

   by completing the square. (4)

---

7. A sequence is given
   750, 740, 730, 720, ...

   (a) Name the type of the sequence and justify your conclusion. (2)

   (b) Write down the nth term of the sequence. (3)

(c) Evaluate the sum of the first 50 terms. **(3)**

(d) Work out the smallest number of terms for the sum of the terms to be negative. **(4)**

---

8. A curve with equation $y = x^2 - 1$ is intersected with a line $y - x = 2$. Calculate the exact coordinates of the points of intersections. **(8)**

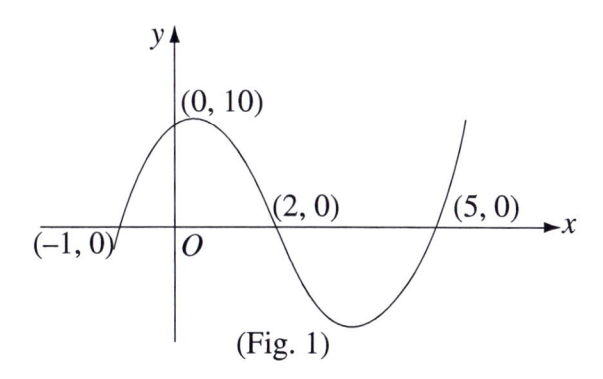

---

9. If $y = f(x)$

(Fig. 1)

Sketch separately the following graphs:

(a) $f(x) - 1$ **(4)**
(b) $f(x - 1)$ **(4)**
(c) $-f(x)$. **(4)**

---

10. The curve shown in Fig.1 is given by $f(x) = x^3 - 6x^2 + 3x + 10$. Find
(a) (i) $f'(x)$ and $f''(x)$. **(4)**

(b) The coordinates of the turning points. **(6)**

TOTAL FOR PAPER: 75 MARKS

GCE Examinations
Advanced Subsidiary

Test Paper 9 SOLUTIONS

Core Mathematics C1
Time: 1 hour 30 minutes

Instructions and Information

Candidates are not allowed to use calculators for this paper.

Full marks are awarded for answers to ALL questions.

This paper has ten questions.

You can start working with any question and you must label clearly all parts.

1. (a) $u_n = 2 + 3^n$
$u_1 = 2 + 3^1 = 5$
$u_2 = 2 + 3^2 = 11$
$u_3 = 2 + 3^3 = 29$
$u_4 = 2 + 3^4 = 83$
$u_5 = 2 + 3^5 = 245.$

(b) $\sum_{n=1}^{5} u_n = \sum_{n=1}^{5} (2 + 3^n)$
$= 5 + 11 + 29 + 83 + 245$
$= 373.$

(c) The common difference is not the same, since $11 - 5 = 6$, $29 - 11 = 18$, $83 - 29 = 54$ are not the same.

(d) $u_{n+1} - u_n = 2 + 3^{n+1} - (2 + 3^n)$
$= 3^{n+1} - 3^n$
$= 3^n(3 - 1)$
$= 2 \times 3^n.$

---

2. $\dfrac{5}{\sqrt{50}} = \dfrac{5}{\sqrt{2}\sqrt{25}} = \dfrac{1}{\sqrt{2}} \times \dfrac{\sqrt{2}}{\sqrt{2}} = \dfrac{1}{2}\sqrt{2}.$

---

3. (a) $x^2(x - 1) > 0 \quad \therefore x > 1$ since $x^2 > 0$

(b) $x(x - 1) > 0$
$x < 0, x > 1.$

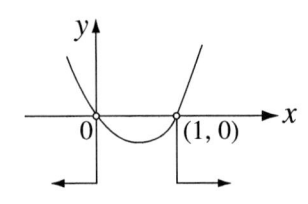

4. (a) $a^6 = 64 \times 16^3 = 2^6 \times (2^4)^3 = 2^6 \times 2^{12} = 2^{18} = (2^3)^6$
$\Rightarrow a = 2^3 = 8$.
(b) $b = \left(\frac{32}{243}\right)^{-\frac{2}{5}} = \left(\frac{243}{32}\right)^{\frac{2}{5}} = \left(\frac{3^5}{2^5}\right)^{\frac{2}{5}} = \left(\frac{3}{2}\right)^2$
$= \frac{9}{4}$.

---

5. (a) $\int \frac{3x^3}{4} dx = \frac{3x^4}{16} + c$.

(b) $\int \frac{x^2-1}{x+1} dx = \int \frac{(x-1)(x+1)}{x+1} dx = \int (x-1) dx$
$= \frac{x^2}{2} - x + c$.

---

6. $x^2 + 25x + 24 = 0$
$\left(x + \frac{25}{2}\right)^2 - \frac{625}{4} + 24 = 0$
$\left(x + \frac{25}{2}\right)^2 - \frac{529}{4} = 0$
$\left(x + \frac{25}{2}\right)^2 - \left(\frac{23}{2}\right)^2 = 0$
$\left(x + \frac{25}{2} - \frac{23}{2}\right)\left(x + \frac{25}{2} + \frac{23}{2}\right) = 0$
$(x + 1)(x + 24) = 0$.

---

7. (a) The sequence is an arithmetic sequence since $740 - 750 = -10$, $730 - 740 = -10$, the common difference is the same and is equal to -10.

(b) $T_n = a + (n - 1)d$
$= 750 + (n - 1)(-10)$
$= 750 - 10n + 10$
$= 760 - 10n$.

(c) $S_{50} = \frac{50}{2}[2 \times 750 + (50 - 1)(-10)]$
$= 25(1500 - 490)$
$= 25(1010) = 25250$.

(d) $S_n = \frac{n}{2}[2a + (n-1)d]$
$\frac{n}{2}[2 \times 750 + (n-1)(-10)]$
$= 750n + n(n-1)(-5) < 0$
$750n - 5n^2 + 5n < 0$
$5n^2 - 755 > 0$
$n^2 - 151 > 0$
$(n - \sqrt{151})(n + \sqrt{151}) > 0$
$\therefore n = 13$

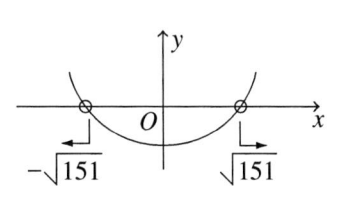

8.

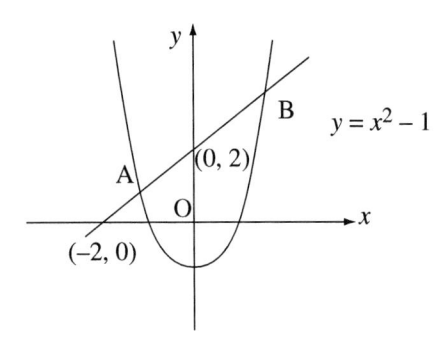

$y = x + 2$
$x^2 - 1 = x + 2$
$x^2 - x - 3 = 0$
$x = \frac{1 \pm \sqrt{1+12}}{2} = \frac{1 \pm \sqrt{13}}{2}$
$x = \frac{1-\sqrt{13}}{2}, x = \frac{1+\sqrt{13}}{2}$
$y = \left(\frac{1-\sqrt{13}}{2}\right)^2 - 1 = \frac{1-2\sqrt{13}+13}{4} - 1$
$= \frac{14-2\sqrt{13}-4}{4} = \frac{10-2\sqrt{13}}{4} = \frac{5}{2} - \frac{1}{2}\sqrt{13}$
$y = \left(\frac{1+\sqrt{13}}{2}\right)^2 - 1 = \frac{1+2\sqrt{13}+13}{4} - 1$
$= \frac{10+2\sqrt{13}}{4} = \frac{5}{2} + \frac{1}{2}\sqrt{13}$
$A\left(\frac{1-\sqrt{13}}{2}, \frac{5}{2} - \frac{1}{2}\sqrt{13}\right) \quad B\left(\frac{1+\sqrt{13}}{2}, \frac{5}{2} + \frac{1}{2}\sqrt{13}\right).$

9. (a)

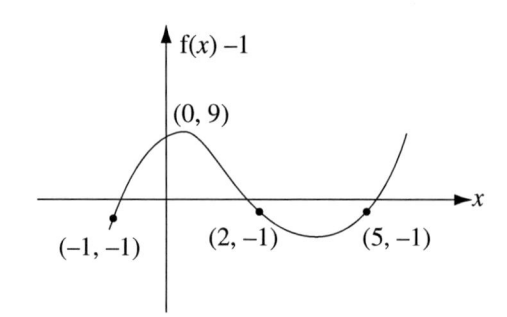

$f(x) - 1$

(0, 9)

(−1, −1) (2, −1) (5, −1)

(b)

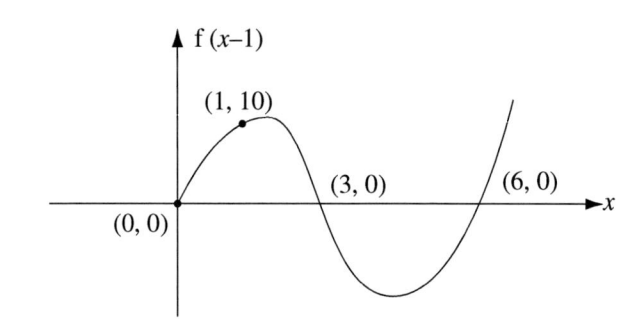

$f(x-1)$

(1, 10)

(0, 0) (3, 0) (6, 0)

(c)

$f(x)$

(−1, 0) (2, 0) (5, 0)

(0, −10)

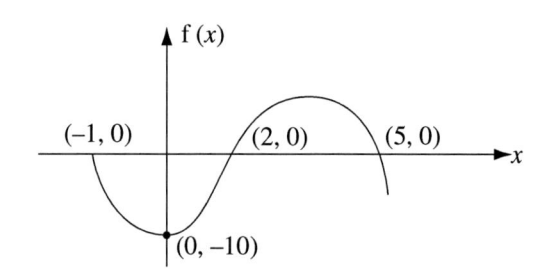

10. (a) $f(x) = x^3 - 6x^2 + 3x + 10$
  (i) $f'(x) = 3x^2 - 12x + 3$
  (ii) $f''(x) = 6x - 12$.

(b) $f'(x) = 0$ for turning points
$f'(x) = 3x^2 - 12x + 3 = 0$ or $x^2 - 4x + 1 = 0$
$x = \frac{12 \pm \sqrt{144-36}}{6} = \frac{12 \pm \sqrt{108}}{6}$
$= \frac{1}{6}(12 \pm 6\sqrt{3}) = 2 \pm \sqrt{3}$

$f(2+\sqrt{3}) = (2+\sqrt{3})^3 - 6(2+\sqrt{3})^2 + 3(2+\sqrt{3}) + 10$
$= 8 + 3(4\sqrt{3}) + 3(2)(3) + 3\sqrt{3} - 6(4+4\sqrt{3}+3) + 6 + 3\sqrt{3} + 10$
$= 8 + 12\sqrt{3} + 18 + 3\sqrt{3} - 42 - 24\sqrt{3} + 6 + 3\sqrt{3} + 10 = -6\sqrt{3}$
$f(2-\sqrt{3}) = (2-\sqrt{3})^3 - 6(2-\sqrt{3})^2 + 3(2-\sqrt{3}) + 10 = 6\sqrt{3}$

TOTAL FOR PAPER: 75 MARKS

GCE Examinations
Advanced Subsidiary

Test Paper 1

Core Mathematics C2
Time: 1 hour 30 minutes

Instructions and Information

Candidates are allowed to use calculators for this paper.

Full marks are awarded for answers to all questions.

This paper has ten questions.

You can start working with any question and you must label clearly all parts.

1. (a) Prove that if $f(x)$ is divided by $x - a$, the remainder is $f(a)$. (3)
   (b) Factorise $f(x) = x^2 - 3x + 2$, using the factor theorem. (3)

2. Determine the coordinates of the centre of the circle and its radius
$$x^2 - 2x + y^2 - 4y - 4 = 0.$$ (4)

3. (a) Prove that the sum of the finite geometric series, $a, ar, ar^2, \ldots ar^{n-1}$ is given by $S_n = \frac{a(r^n - 1)}{r - 1}$ where $|r| > 1$. (4)
   (b) If $1, 2, 2^2, 2^3 \ldots$ Find S_{10}. (3)

4. (a) Write down the first four terms, an ascending powers of x, of the binomial expansion of $(1 + ax)^8$, where a is a non-zero constant. (2)

   Given that in the expansion of $(1 + ax)^8$, the coefficient of x is $(-b)$ and the coefficient of x^2 is $7b$.

   (b) Find the value of a and the value b. (4)

5. (a) Prove the formula $s = r\theta$ where s is the length of arc in metre; r, the radius in metres and θ the angle in radians subtending the arc s. (2)
   (b) Prove the area of a sector is $A = \frac{1}{2}r^2\theta$. (3)

6. Sketch the following graphs:
   (i) $f(x) = \sin x$ (2)
   (ii) $2f(x)$ (2)

(iii) $f\left(x + \frac{\pi}{2}\right)$ (2)

(iv) $f(2x)$ (2)

for $0 \leq x \leq 2\pi$.

---

7. Solve

   (a) $3^x = 15$, giving your answer to 3 significant figures, (3)

   (b) $\log_5(2x + 3) = \log_5 x + \log_5 17$. (3)

---

8. Evaluate $\int_0^1 \sqrt{2x + 1}\,dx$ for four intervals using the trapezium rule, giving your answer to approximate three decimal places. (6)

---

9. A square metal sheet of 1 m side is cut at the four corners as shown in Fig. 1.

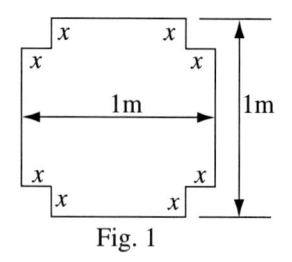

Fig. 1

Show that the volume of the cuboid, by turning up the four sides is given by

$$V = 4x^3 - 4x^2 + x = f(x)$$ (2)

Determine (i) $f'(x)$ (ii) $f''(x)$. (2)

Find the turning points of the functions f(x), hence deduce the value of x which gives a maximum volume hence check your answer by considering the second derivative. **(3)**

Find the exact maximum volume, in m³ and the number of litres to the nearest integer. **(4)**

---

10. (a) Sketch the quadratic function $y = (x-3)^2 + 4$. **(4)**

(b) The curve is intersected by the straight line with equation $x + y = 19$. Find the coordinates of the points of intersections.
Determine the exact area between the curve and the line. **(6)**

TOTAL FOR PAPER: 75 MARKS

GCE Examinations
Advanced Subsidiary

Test Paper 1 Solutions

Core Mathematics C2
Time: 1 hour 30 minutes

Instructions and Information

Candidates are allowed to use calculators for this paper.

Full marks are awarded for answers to ALL questions.

This paper has ten questions.

You can start working with any question and you must label clearly all parts.

1. (a) $\frac{f(x)}{x-a} = Q(x) + \frac{R}{x-a}$ ... (1)

where $Q(x)$ is an equation of one degree less than $f(x)$ and R is the remainder.

Multiplying each term of (1) by $x - a$

$\frac{f(x)}{x-a}(x-a) = Q(x)(x-a) + \frac{R}{x-a}(x-a)$

$f(x) = Q(x)(x-a) + R.$

If $x = a$, then $f(a) = Q(a)(a-a) + R$

$\therefore R = f(a).$

(b) $f(x) = x^2 - 3x + 2$

if $x = 1$, then $f(1) = 1 - 3 + 2 = 0$, therefore

$x - 1$ is a factor.

$$\begin{array}{r}
x - 2 \\
x-1 \overline{\smash{\big)}\, x^2 - 3x + 2}\\
\underline{x^2 - x}\\
-2x + 2\\
\underline{-2x + 2}\\
0
\end{array}$$

$f(x) = x^2 - 3x + 2 = (x-1)(x-2).$

---

2. $x^2 - 2x + y^2 - 4y - 4 = 0$

using the method of completing the square, we have

$(x-1)^2 - 1 + (y-2)^2 - 4 - 4 = 0$

$(x-1)^2 + (y-2)^2 = 3^2 \quad \therefore C(1, 2), r = 3.$

---

3. (a) $S_n = a + ar + ar^2 + \cdots + ar^{n-1} \ldots (1)$

multiplying both sides by r

$rS_n = ar + ar^2 + ar^3 + \quad +ar^n \ldots (2)$

$(2)-(1)$

$rS_n - S_n = ar^n - a$

$S_n(r-1) = a(r^n - 1)$

$S_n = \dfrac{a(r^n - 1)}{r - 1} \qquad |r| > 1.$

(b) $S_{10} = \dfrac{1(2^{10} - 1)}{2 - 1} = 2^{10} - 1$

$= 1024 - 1 = 1023.$

---

4. (a) $(1 + ax)^8 = 1 + 8ax + \dfrac{8 \times 7}{1 \times 2}a^2x^2 + \dfrac{8 \times 7 \times 6}{1 \times 2 \times 3}a^3x^3$

$= 1 + 8ax + 28a^2x^2 + 56a^3x^3$

(b) $\quad 8a = -b$

$28a^2 = 7b$

$\dfrac{28a^2}{8a} = -\dfrac{7b}{b}$

$\dfrac{4a^2}{8a} = -1$

$4a^2 = -8a \Rightarrow 4a(a + 2) = 0$

$a = 0 \quad \text{and} \quad a = -2, b = 16.$

5. (a)

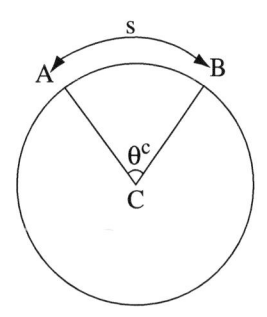

The circumference of a circle is given as $2\pi r$, $s = 2\pi r \left(\frac{\theta^c}{2\pi}\right) = r\theta^c$ where θ^c is a portion of the angle at the centre.

(b) The area of a circle is πr^2, the area of the sector, ABC is $A = \pi r^2 \times \frac{\theta^c}{2\pi} = \frac{1}{2}r^2\theta^c$.

6. (i)

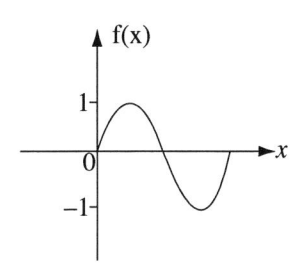

(ii)

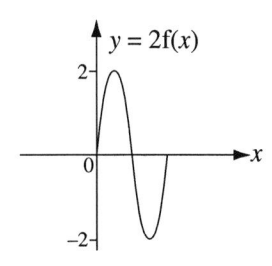

(iii)

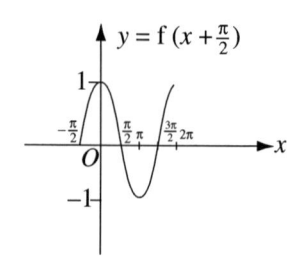

Graph of $y = f(x + \frac{\pi}{2})$

(iv)

Graph of $y = f(2x)$

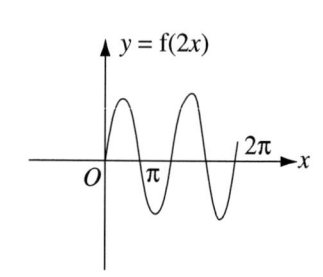

7. (a) $3^x = 15$

taking logarithms to the base 10 on both sides

$\log_{10} 3^x = \log_{10} 15 \Rightarrow x \log_{10} 3 = \log_{10} 15$

$x = \dfrac{\log_{10} 15}{\log_{10} 3} = \dfrac{1.176091259}{0.477121254} = 2.46497352$

$= 2.46$ to 3s.f.

(b) $\log_5(2x+3) = \log_5 x + \log_5 17$

$\log_5(2x+3) - \log_5 x = \log_5 17$

$\log_5 \frac{2x+3}{x} = \log_5 17$

$\therefore \frac{2x+3}{x} = 17$

$2x + 3 = 17x$

$15x = 3$

$x = \frac{3}{15} = \frac{1}{5}.$

---

8. $\int_0^1 \sqrt{2x+1}\,dx \approx \frac{h}{2}[y_0 + 2y_1 + 2y_2 + 2y_3 + y_4]$

x	0	0.25	0.5	0.75	1
$y = \sqrt{2x+1}$	1	$\sqrt{1.5}$	$\sqrt{2}$	$\sqrt{2.5}$	$\sqrt{3}$

$h = 0.25$

$\int_0^1 \sqrt{2x+1}\,dx \approx \frac{0.25}{2}[1 + 2(\sqrt{1.5} + \sqrt{2} + \sqrt{2.5}) + \sqrt{3}]$

$= 0.125[1 + 2(4.220097264) + 1.732050808]$

$= 1.396530667$

$= 1.397$

---

9. $V = (1-2x)^2 x = (1 - 4x + 4x^2)x = 4x^3 - 4x^2 + x = f(x)$

(i) $f'(x) = 12x^2 - 8x + 1$

(ii) $f''(x) = 24x - 8$

$f'(x) = 0$ for turning points

$12x^2 - 8x + 1 = 0$

$x = \frac{8 \pm \sqrt{64-48}}{2 \times 12} = \frac{8 \pm 4}{24}$

$x = \frac{12}{24} = \frac{1}{2}$ or $x = \frac{4}{24} = \frac{1}{6}.$

If we cut $\frac{1}{2}$m from each side there will be nothing left therefore $x = \frac{1}{6}$ is the length required to give the maximum volume $f''\left(\frac{1}{6}\right) = 24\left(\frac{1}{6}\right) - 8 = 4 - 8 = -4 < 0$ which confirms that $= \frac{1}{6}$ gives a maximum.

$V_{max} = 4\left(\frac{1}{6}\right)^3 - 4\left(\frac{1}{6}\right)^2 + \frac{1}{6}$

$= 4 \times \frac{1}{216} - 4 \times \frac{1}{36} + \frac{1}{6}$

$= \frac{1}{54} - \frac{1}{9} + \frac{1}{6}$

$= \frac{1}{54} - \frac{6}{54} + \frac{9}{54} = \frac{4}{54}$

$= \frac{2}{27}\text{m}^3 = 74.07407407$

$= 74$ litres to the nearest integer.

10.

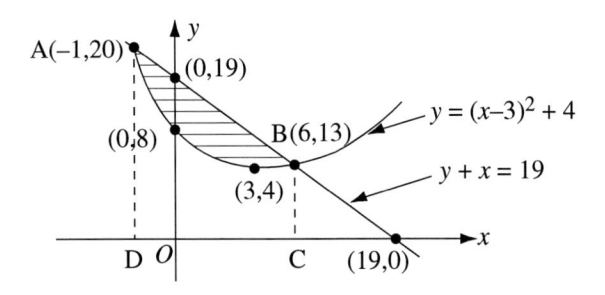

$(x-3)^2 + 4 = y = 19 - x$

$x^2 - 6x + 9 + 4 = 19 - x \Rightarrow x^2 - 5x - 6 = 0$

$(x - 6)(x + 1) = 0$

$x = -1$, or $x = 6$

$y = 20$, or $y = 13$.

The area under the curve is given by

$$\int_{-1}^{6}(x^2 - 6x + 13)\,dx = \left[\frac{x^3}{3} - \frac{6x^2}{2} + 13x\right]_{-1}^{6}$$

$$= \left[\frac{216}{3} - 3(36) + 78\right] - \left[-\frac{1}{3} - 3 - 13\right]$$

$$= 72 - 108 + 78 + 16\frac{1}{3} = 58\frac{1}{3}\text{ s.u.}$$

The area of the trapezium ABCD $= \dfrac{(20 + 13) \times 7}{2}$

$$= 115\frac{1}{2}\text{ s.u.}$$

The shaded area $= 115\frac{1}{2} - 58\frac{1}{3}$

$$= \frac{231}{2} - \frac{175}{3}$$

$$= \frac{231 \times 3 - 175 \times 2}{6} = \frac{693 - 350}{6}$$

$$= \frac{343}{6} = 57\frac{1}{6}\text{ s.u.}$$

TOTAL FOR PAPER: 75 MARKS

GCE Examinations
Advanced Subsidiary

Test Paper 2

Core Mathematics C2
Time: 1 hour 30 minutes

Instructions and Information

Candidates are allowed to use calculators for this paper.

Full marks are awarded for answers to ALL questions.

This paper has ten questions.

You can start working with any question and you must label clearly all parts.

1. (a) Prove that if $f(x)$ is divided by $x + a$, the remainder is $f(-a)$. **(3)**

    (b) Show that, if $f(x) = x^2 - 3x + 2 = 0$ when $x = 1$, then $x - 1$ is a factor of $f(x)$. **(3)**

---

2. Determine the coordinates of the centre and its radius of the circle $x^2 - 4x + y^2 - 6y - 3 = 0$. **(4)**

---

3. A finite geometric series is given $a, ar, ar^2, \ldots, ar^{n-1}$.

    Determine the sum to infinity given that the series converges. **(4)**

---

4. (a) Find the first 3 terms, in ascending powers of x, of the binomial expansion

    $$(1 + ax)^7,$$

    where a is a constant **(2)**

    The first 3 terms are $1, 42x$ and bx^2, where b is a constant.

    (b) Find the value of a and the value of b. **(4)**

5. Fig.1 shows the shaded area of the segment, where $r = 15\,\text{cm}$.

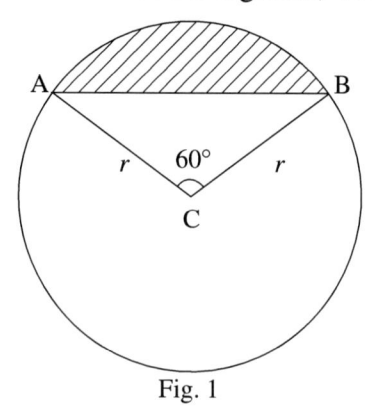

Fig. 1

Determine:

(a) The length of the chord, AB, (3)

(b) The area of the triangle $\triangle ABC$, (3)

(c) the area of the sector ABC, (3)

(d) the area of the segment. (3)

---

6. Sketch the following graphs:

   (i) $f(x) = \cos x$ (2)

   (ii) $f\left(x - \dfrac{\pi}{2}\right)$ (2)

   (iii) $-f(x)$ (2)

   (iv) $f\left(\dfrac{x}{2}\right)$ (2)

   for $0 \leq x \leq 2\pi$.

---

7. (a) Sketch the graphs:

   (i) $y = 2^x$ (ii) $y = 3^x$ (iii) $y = a^x, \; 2 < a < 3$. (3)

(b) Solve $5^x = 7$ (3)

(c) Simplify $3 \log x^2 + 5 \log x - 3 \log x$. (3)

---

8. The cross-sectional area of an object is given $\int_0^{10} \sqrt{10-x}\, dx$.

    (a) Complete the table below, giving values of y to 3 decimal places.

x	0	2	4	6	8	10
y	3.162	2.878		2		0

    (2)

    (b) Use the trapezium rule with all the values in the table to estimate this crossectional area. (4)

---

9. Sketch the quadratic function
$$f(x) = y = (x+2)^2 - 5.$$
(2)

    (a) Show by calculus that the minimum value is given by the coordinates $(-2, -5)$. (4)

    (b) Evaluate the exact area between the graph and the axes. (6)

---

10. It is required to sketch the cubic function
$$y = f(x) = x^3 + 9x^2 + 23x + 15.$$
(5)

    Factorise $f(x)$, given that $f(-1) = 0$, hence sketch the graph and find the coordinates of the turning points, justifying the minimum and maximum, to 3 s.f., and insert all the values of the coordinates of the turning points and the points of the intersections with the axes. (10)

TOTAL FOR PAPER: 75 MARKS

GCE Examinations
Advanced Subsidiary

Test Paper 2 Solutions

Core Mathematics C2
Time: 1 hour 30 minutes

Instructions and Information

Candidates are allowed to use calculators for this paper.

Full marks are awarded for answers to ALL questions.

This paper has ten questions.

You can start working with any question and you must label clearly all parts.

1. (a) $\dfrac{f(x)}{x+a} = Q(x) + \dfrac{R}{x+a}$ ... (1)

   Multiplying each term of (1) by $x+a$, then $f(x) = Q(x)(x+a) + R$, if $x = -a$, then $\boxed{f(-a) = R}$

   (b) $f(1) = 1^2 - 3(1) + 2 = 0$

   $R = f(1) = 0$, therefore $x - 1$ is a factor.

2. $x^2 - 4x + y^2 - 6y - 3 = 0$

   using the method of completing the square, we have

   $(x - 2)^2 - 4 + (y - 3)^2 - 9 - 3 = 0$

   $(x - 2)^2 + (y - 3)^2 = 4^2.$

3. $S_n = a + ar + ar^2 + \cdots + ar^{n-1}$ ... (1)

   multiplying both sides by r

   $rS_n = ar + ar^2 + \cdots + ar^n$ ... (2)

   Since the series converges, $|r| < 1$,

   $\therefore S_n - rS_n = a - ar^n$

   $S_n = \dfrac{a(1 - r^n)}{1 - r}$

   $|r|^\infty \to 0$ as $|r| < 1$

   $\boxed{S_\infty = \dfrac{a}{1 - r}}.$

4. (a) $(1 + ax)^7 = 1 + 7ax + \dfrac{7 \times 6}{1 \times 2} a^2 x^2.$

(b) $7ax = 42x$ by equating coefficients

$$\boxed{a = 6}$$

$21a^2 = b$

$b = 21 \times 36$

$$\boxed{b = 756.}$$

---

5. (a)

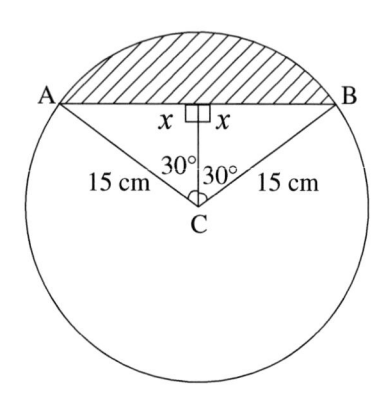

$\sin 30° = \dfrac{x}{15}$

$x = 15 \sin 30°$

$ = 15 \times 0.5 = 7.5$ cm

$\therefore$ AB $= 2x = 15$ cm.

Alternatively $\widehat{CAB} = \widehat{CBA} = 60°$, therefore $\triangle ABC$ is equilateral, therefore AB $= 15$ cm.

(b) Area of $\triangle ABC = \dfrac{1}{2}r^2 \sin \theta$

$ = \dfrac{1}{2}(15)^2 \sin 60° = \dfrac{225}{4}\sqrt{3} = 97.4$ cm²

$$= \frac{1}{2}r^2\theta = \frac{1}{2}(15)^2\frac{\pi}{3} = 117.80937245$$
$$= 118 \text{ cm}^2 \text{ to 3s.f.}$$

(d) Area of segment = area of sector − area of △ A B C

$$= 117.8 - 97.4 = 20.4 \text{ cm}^2 \text{ to 3s.f.}$$

---

6. (i)

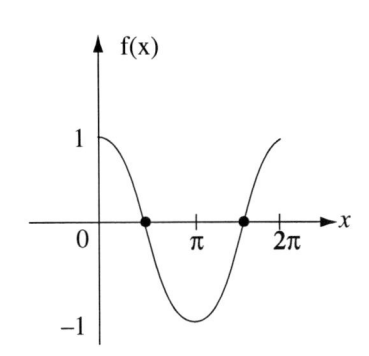

[Graph of $f(x)$ showing a cosine-like curve starting at 1, crossing zero between 0 and π, reaching −1 minimum, crossing zero between π and 2π, returning toward 1]

(ii)

[Graph of $f(x-\frac{\pi}{2})$ showing the curve shifted right by π/2, starting at 0, peaking at 1, crossing zero at π, reaching −1, crossing zero at 2π]

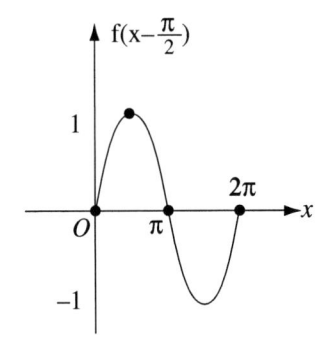

(iii)

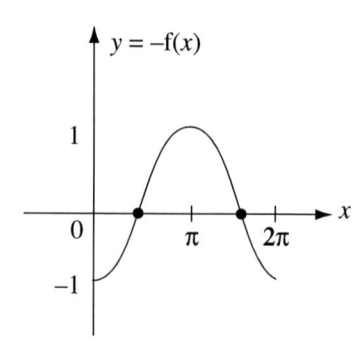

$y = -f(x)$

(iv)

$f(\frac{x}{2})$

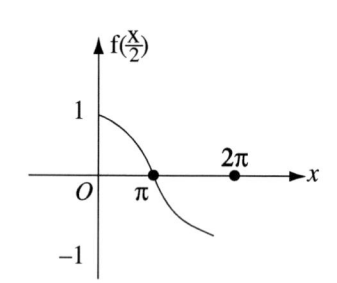

7. (a)

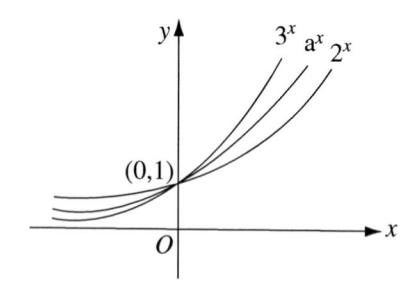

(b) $5^x = 7$

$x \log 5 = \log 7$

$x = \dfrac{\log 7}{\log 5}$

$= 1.209061455$

$= 1.21$ to 3 s.f.

(c) $3 \log x^2 + 5 \log x - 3 \log x^3$

$= \log x^6 + \log x^5 - \log x^9$

$= \log x^{11} - \log x^9$

$= \log x^2.$

---

8. (a)

x	0	2	4	6	8	10
y	3.162	2.828	2.449	2	1.414	0

(b) $\int_0^{10} \sqrt{(10-x)}\ dx \approx \dfrac{h}{2}[3.162 + 2(2.828 + 2.449 + 2 + 1.414) + 0] = 20.6$ s.u.

Coordinates on the x-axis $(-2-\sqrt{5},\ 0)$ and $(-2+\sqrt{5},\ 0)$

9.

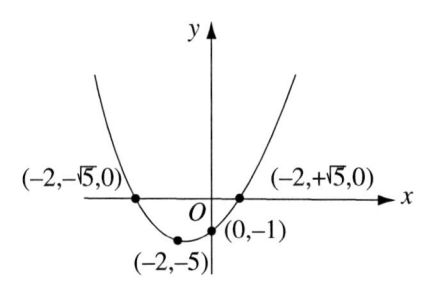

(a) $y = (x+2)^2 - 5 = f(x)$

$\dfrac{dy}{dx} = 2(x+2) = f'(x)$

$\dfrac{dy}{dx} = 0$ for turning points

$2(x+2) = 0$

$x = -2$

$f''(x) = \dfrac{d^2y}{dx^2} = 2 > 0$ thus giving a minimum

$y_{min} = -5$

∴ $(-2, -5)$ are the coordinates of the minimum point

(b) $f(0) = -1$

$f(x) = 0, (x+2)^2 - 5 = 0$

$x = -2 \pm \sqrt{5}$

$\displaystyle\int_{-2-\sqrt{5}}^{-2+\sqrt{5}} \left[(x+2)^2 - 5\right] dx = \left[\dfrac{(x+2)^3}{3} - 5x\right]_{-2-\sqrt{5}}^{-2+\sqrt{5}}$

$= \dfrac{(-2+\sqrt{5}+2)^3}{3} - 5(-2+\sqrt{5}) - \left\{\dfrac{(-2-\sqrt{5}+2)^3}{3} - 5(-2-\sqrt{5})\right\}$

$= \dfrac{5\sqrt{5}}{3} + 10 - 5\sqrt{5} + \dfrac{5\sqrt{5}}{3} - 10 - 5\sqrt{5} = \dfrac{10\sqrt{5}}{3} - 10\sqrt{5}$

$= \dfrac{10\sqrt{5}}{3} - \dfrac{30\sqrt{5}}{3} = \dfrac{-20\sqrt{5}}{3}$

the negative sign indicates that the area is below the x-axis.

Therefore the exact area required is $\dfrac{20\sqrt{5}}{3}$.

10. $f(x) = x^3 + 9x^2 + 23x + 15$

$$\begin{array}{r} x^2 + 8x + 15 \\ x+1\overline{\smash{\big)}\,x^3 + 9x^2 + 23x + 15} \\ \underline{x^3 + x^2 } \\ 8x^2 + 23x + 15 \\ \underline{8x^2 + 8x } \\ 15x + 15 \\ \underline{15x + 15} \\ 0 \end{array}$$

$f(x) = (x+1)(x^2 + 8x + 15) = (x+1)(x+3)(x+5)$

$f'(x) = 3x^2 + 18x + 23 = 0$

$$x = \frac{-18 \pm \sqrt{324 - 276}}{6}$$

$$= \frac{-18 \pm \sqrt{48}}{6}$$

$$= -\frac{18}{6} \pm \frac{4}{6}\sqrt{3}$$

$$= -3 \pm \frac{2}{3}\sqrt{3}$$

$x = -4.15$ or -1.85 to 3s.f.

$f''(x) = 6x + 18$, $f''(-4.15) < 0$ maximum

$f''(-1.85) > 0$ minimum.

```
           y ▲
           │ (0,15)
  (-4.15,3.08)
      •    │
    ┼──┼──┼──┼──┤   O
    -5 -4 -3 -2 -1      ─────► x
         •
    (-1.85,-3.08)
```

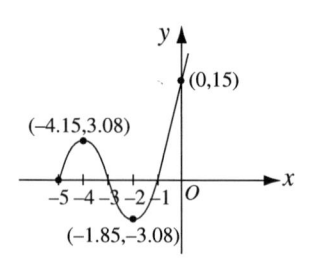

$$f(-2) = (-1)(1)(3) = -3$$
$$f(-4) = (-3)(-1)(1) = 3$$
$$f(-4.15) = (-4.15)^3 + 9(-4.15)^2 + 23(-4.15) + 15$$
$$= 3.08 \text{ to 3s.f.}$$
$$f(-1.85) = (-1.85)^3 + 9(-1.85)^2 + 23(-1.85) + 15$$
$$= -3.08 \text{ to 3s.f.}$$

TOTAL FOR PAPER: 75 MARKS

GCE Examinations
Advanced Subsidiary

Test Paper 3

Core Mathematics C2
Time: 1 hour 30 minutes

Instructions and Information

Candidates are allowed to use calculators for this paper.

Full marks are awarded for answers to ALL questions.

This paper has ten questions.

You can start working with any question and you must label clearly all parts.

1. Factorise the cubic expressions:
   (a) $f(x) = x^3 + 3x^2 - 4$ (3)
   (b) $g(x) = 6x^3 + 11x^2 - x - 6$ (3)
   hence solve $f(x) = 0$, $g(x) = 0$. (4)

---

2. (a) Prove the formula of the circle
$$(x - a)^2 + (y - b)^2 = r^2.$$ (3)
   (b) If the coordinates of the centre of a circle are $(-f, -g)$ and the radius r, show that the equation of the circle is
$$x^2 + 2fx + y^2 + 2gy + c = 0.$$ (3)
   where $c = f^2 + g^2 - r^2$.

---

3. (a) The salary of a teacher at the beginning of his carreer is £18000, assuming an increase of salary of 5%, determine the salary in the fortieth year of the service, to the nearest £100. (3)
   (b) How much gross salary has he or she received in forty years, to the nearest £1000. (3)

---

4. Find the coefficient of x^7 in the expansion $(1 + x)^{35}$. (4)

5. Fig.1 shows a scalere triangle, ABC.

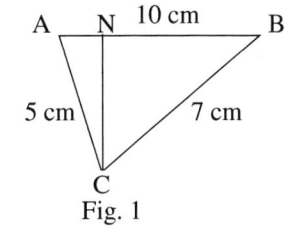

Fig. 1

Determine:

(a) the angles A, B and C (4)

(b) the area of △ABC (2)

(c) the perpendicular distance CN. (2)

---

6. (a) Solve $\sin\left(x - \frac{\pi}{2}\right) = \frac{1}{2}$ for $0 < x < 2\pi$. (3)

(b) Solve $\tan 2x = 1$ for $90° < x < 270°$. (3)

(c) Solve the equation
$$\sin^2\left(x + \frac{\pi}{6}\right) = \frac{1}{2} \text{ for } -\pi \leq x < \pi.$$ (4)

---

7. (a) Express $\log_{25} x$ in the form $k \log_5 x$ stating the value of k. (3)

(b) A geometric series is given
$$\log_5 x + \log_{25} x + \log_{625} x + \ldots$$
Find the sum to infinity. (5)

---

8. For the quadratic function $f(x) = ax^2 + bx + c$, determine the condition for turning points and justify the maximum and minimum points, illustrating with curves the answers. (5)

Hence find the nature of the curves (i) $-x^2 - 3x + 1$
(ii) $x^2 + 4x - 1$
and their coordinates of the maximum or minimum points. **(5)**

---

9. (a) Sketch the curve
$$f(x) = (x - 1)(x - 3)^2.$$ **(2)**

(b) Determine (i) $f'(x)$ and (ii) $f''(x)$. **(2)**

(c) Find the turning points. **(2)**

(d) Determine the nature of the curve and insert the coordinates on the curve. **(1)**

---

10. Evaluate the exact areas; (i) between the curve $f(x) = (x - 1)(x - 3)^2$ and the axes and (ii) between the curve and the x-axis. **(6)**

TOTAL FOR PAPER: 75 MARKS

GCE Examinations
Advanced Subsidiary

Test Paper 3 Solutions

Core Mathematics C2
Time: 1 hour 30 minutes

Instructions and Information

Candidates are allowed to use calculators for this paper.

Full marks are awarded for answers to ALL questions.

This paper has ten questions.

You can start working with any question and you must label clearly all parts.

1. (a) $f(x) = x^3 + 3x^2 - 4$
$f(1) = 1^3 + 3(1)^2 - 4 = 1 + 3 - 4 = 0$
therefore $x - 1$ is a factor of $f(x)$

$$\begin{array}{r}
x^2+4x+4 \\
x-1{\overline{\smash{\big)}\,x^3+3x^2-4}} \\
\underline{x^3-x^2} \\
4x^2-4 \\
\underline{4x^2-4x} \\
4x-4 \\
\underline{4x-4} \\
0
\end{array}$$

$f(x) = (x-1)(x^2 + 4x + 4)$
$= (x-1)(x+2)^2$

(b) $g(x) = 6x^3 + 11x^2 - x - 6$
$g(-1) = -6 + 11 + 1 - 6 = 0$
$\therefore \quad x + 1$ is a factor of $g(x)$

$$\begin{array}{r}
6x^2+5x-6 \\
x+1{\overline{\smash{\big)}\,6x^3+11x^2-x-6}} \\
\underline{6x^3+6x^2} \\
5x^2-x-6 \\
\underline{5x^2+5x} \\
-6x-6 \\
\underline{-6x-6} \\
0
\end{array}$$

$g(x) = (x+1)(6x^2 + 5x - 6)$
$= (x+1)(2x+3)(3x-2)$

(c) $f(x) = (x-1)(x+2)^2 = 0$
$x = 1 \quad$ or $\quad x = -2 \quad$ twice

$g(x) = (x+1)(2x+3)(3x-2)$
$x = -1 \quad$ or $\quad x = -\frac{3}{2} \quad$ or $\quad x = \frac{2}{3}$.

2. (a)

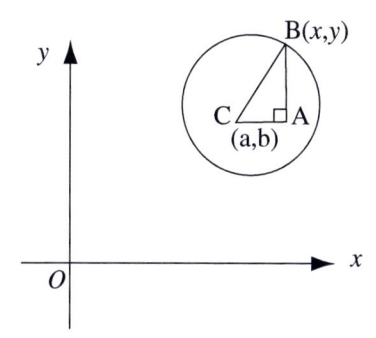

$AC = x - a$
$AB = y - b$
using Pythagoras's theorem $= r^2$.
$(x - a)^2 + (y - b)^2 = r^2$

(b) $(x + f)^2 + (y + g)^2 = r^2$
$x^2 + 2fx + f^2 + y^2 + 2gy + g^2 - r^2 = 0$
$x^2 + 2fx + y^2 + 2gy + f^2 + g^2 - r^2 = 0$
$x^2 + 2fx + y^2 + 2gy + c = 0$
where $c = f^2 + g^2 - r^2$.

---

3. (a) £18000, 18000×1.05, 18000×1.05^2, ... 18000×1.05^{39}
$T_{40} = £18000 \times 1.05^{39} = 120685.5208$
$= £120700$ to the nearest £100.

(b) $S_{40} = 18000 \times \frac{1.05^{40}-1}{1.05-1} = 2174395.936$
$= £2174000$ to the nearest £1000.

---

4. $(1 + x)^{35} = 1 + \binom{35}{1} x + \cdots + x^{35}$.

The coefficient of x^7 is $\binom{35}{7} = \frac{35!}{28!7!} = 6724520$.

5. (a) $a^2 = b^2 + c^2 - 2bc \cos \hat{A}$ the cosine rule

$2bc \cos \hat{A} = b^2 + c^2 - a^2$

$\cos \hat{A} = \frac{b^2 + c^2 - a^2}{2bc}$

$= \frac{5^2 + 10^2 - 7^2}{2 \times 5 \times 10}$

$= \frac{125 - 49}{100} = \frac{76}{100} = 0.76$

$\hat{A} = 40.53580211°$

$= 40.5°$ to 3s.f.

similarly

$b^2 = a^2 + c^2 - 2ac \cos \hat{B}$

$\cos \hat{B} = \frac{a^2 + c^2 - b^2}{2ac}$

$= \frac{7^2 + 10^2 - 5^2}{2 \times 7 \times 10}$

$= \frac{149 - 25}{140} = \frac{124}{140} = 0.885714285$

$\hat{B} = 27.6604499°$

$\hat{B} = 27.7°$ to 3s.f.

$\therefore \hat{C} = 180° - 40.53580211° - 27.6604499°$

$= 111.803748°$

$= 112°$ to 3s.f.

(b) Area $\triangle ABC = \frac{1}{2} 5 \times 7 \times \sin 111.803748°$

$= 16.24807681$

$= 16.2 \text{cm}^2$ to 3 s.f.

(c) $\frac{CN \times AB}{2} = 16.24807681$

$\therefore CN = 3.25$ cm to 3 s.f.

6. (a) $\sin\left(x - \frac{\pi}{2}\right) = \frac{1}{2}$ for $0 < x < 2\pi$.
$$= \sin\frac{\pi}{6} = \sin\frac{5\pi}{6}$$
$$x - \frac{\pi}{2} = \frac{\pi}{6} \Rightarrow x = \frac{\pi}{2} + \frac{\pi}{6} = \frac{4\pi}{6} = \frac{2\pi}{3}$$
$$x - \frac{\pi}{2} = \frac{5\pi}{6} \Rightarrow x = \frac{5\pi}{6} + \frac{\pi}{2} = \frac{8\pi}{6} = \frac{4\pi}{3}$$

(b) $\tan 2x = 1$
$$= \tan 45° = \tan 225°$$
$x = 45°$ or $x = 225°$ $x = 22.5°$ or $x = 112.5°$
the only solution is $\boxed{x = 112.5°}$

(c) $\sin^2\left(x + \frac{\pi}{6}\right) = \frac{1}{2}$
square rooting each side
$\sin\left(x + \frac{\pi}{6}\right) = \pm\frac{1}{\sqrt{2}}$
$\sin\left(x + \frac{\pi}{6}\right) = \frac{1}{\sqrt{2}} = \sin\frac{\pi}{4} = \sin\frac{3\pi}{4}$
$x = \frac{\pi}{4} - \frac{\pi}{6} = \frac{3\pi}{12} - \frac{2\pi}{12} = \boxed{\frac{\pi}{12}}$
$x = \frac{3\pi}{4} - \frac{\pi}{6} = \frac{9\pi}{12} - \frac{2\pi}{12} = \boxed{\frac{7\pi}{12}}$
$\sin\left(x + \frac{\pi}{6}\right) = -\frac{1}{\sqrt{2}} = \sin\left(-\frac{\pi}{4}\right) = \sin\left(-\frac{3\pi}{4}\right)$
$x = \boxed{-\frac{5\pi}{12}}$ or $x = \boxed{-\frac{11\pi}{12}}$.

---

7. (a) $\log_{25} x = \frac{\log_5 x}{\log_5 25} = \frac{\log_5 x}{\log_5 5^2} = \frac{\log_5 x}{2\log_5 5}$ ⬅
$$= \frac{1}{2}\log_5 x = k\log_5 x$$
where $k = \frac{1}{2}$.

(b) $\log_5 x + \log_{25} x + \log_{625} x + \ldots$
$$= \log_5 x + \frac{1}{2}\log_5 x + \frac{1}{4}\log_5 x + \ldots$$

$$S_\infty = \frac{a}{1-r} \quad a = \log_5 x \quad r = \frac{\frac{1}{2}\log_5 x}{\log_5 x} = \frac{1}{2}$$

$$S_\infty = \frac{\log_5 x}{1-\frac{1}{2}} = 2\log_5 x$$

$$S_\infty = \log_5 x^2.$$

---

8. $f(x) = ax^2 + bx + c$
$f'(x) = 2ax + b$
$f'(x) = 0$ for turning points
$2ax + b = 0$
$x = -\frac{b}{2a}$
$f''(x) = 2a$
If $a > 0$, $f''(x) > 0$, giving $f(x)_{min}$
If $a < 0$, $f''(x) < 0$, giving $f(x)_{max}$

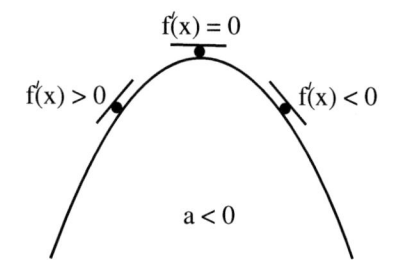

$f''(x) < 0$
the change of the gradient is negative.
(i) $y = -x^2 - 3x + 1$
$\frac{dy}{dx} = -2x - 3$
$\frac{dy}{dx} = 0$ for turning points
$x = -\frac{3}{2}$

$(-\frac{3}{2}, \frac{13}{4})$

$\frac{d^2y}{dx^2} = -2$

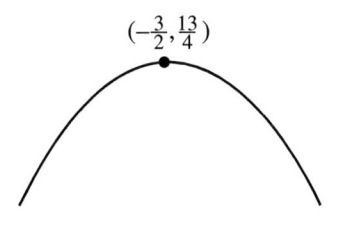

$f\left(\frac{-3}{2}\right) = -\left(\frac{-3}{2}\right)^2 - 3\left(\frac{-3}{2}\right) + 1$

$= -\frac{9}{4} + \frac{9}{2} + 1 \quad = \frac{9}{4} + 1 = \frac{13}{4}$

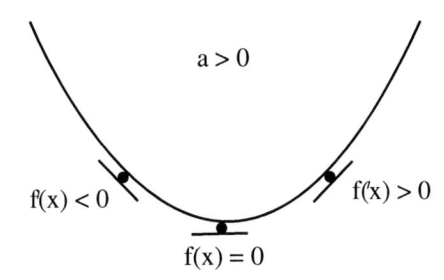

a > 0

f'(x) < 0   f'(x) > 0

f'(x) = 0

the change of the gradient is positive

(ii) $y = x^2 + 4x - 1$

$\frac{dy}{dx} = 2x + 4$

$\frac{dy}{dx} = 0$ for turning points

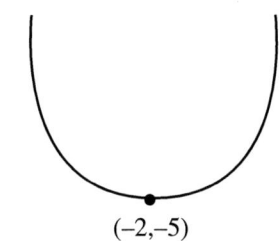

$x = -2 \quad \frac{d^2y}{dx^2} = 2$

$f(-2) = (-2)^2 + 4(-2) - 1$

$= 4 - 8 - 1 = -5$

$(-2, -5)$

9. (a)

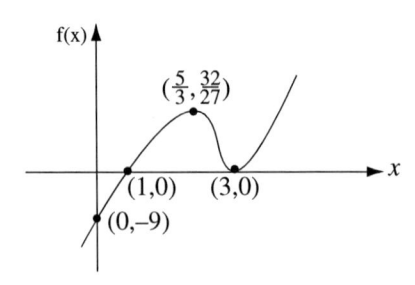

[Graph showing f(x) with points $(\frac{5}{3}, \frac{32}{27})$, $(1,0)$, $(3,0)$, $(0,-9)$]

$f(x) = (x-1)(x-3)^2$
$f(0) = (-1)9$
$ = -9$
$f(x) = 0$
$x = 1$ or $x = 3$ (twice) thus touching the x-axis.

(b) $f(x) = (x-1)(x^2 - 6x + 9)$
$ = x^3 - x^2 - 6x^2 + 6x + 9x - 9$
$ = x^3 - 7x^2 + 15x - 9$
$f'(x) = 3x^2 - 14x + 15$
$f''(x) = 6x - 14$

(c) $f'(x) = 0$
$3x^2 - 14x + 15 = 0$
$x = \frac{14 \pm \sqrt{196 - 180}}{6} = \frac{14 \pm 4}{6}$
$x = \frac{14+4}{6} = 3$ or $x = \frac{10}{6} = \frac{5}{3}$.

(d) $f''(3) = 6(3) - 14 = 4 > 0$ minimum
$f''\left(\frac{5}{3}\right) = 6\left(\frac{5}{3}\right) - 14 = -4 < 0$ maximum
$f(3) = 0$, $f\left(\frac{5}{3}\right) = \left(\frac{5}{3} - 1\right)\left(\frac{5}{3} - 3\right)^2$
$\phantom{f(3) = 0, f\left(\frac{5}{3}\right)} = \frac{2}{3} \times \frac{16}{9} = \frac{32}{27}$.

10.

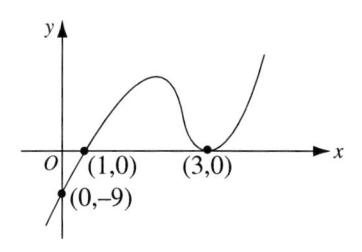

(graph showing curve through (1,0) and (3,0), with y-intercept (0,-9))

(i) $\int_0^1 (x-1)(x-3)^2 dx$

$= \int_0^1 (x^3 - 7x^2 + 15x - 9) dx$

$= \left[\dfrac{x^4}{4} - \dfrac{7}{3}x^3 + \dfrac{15}{2}x^2 - 9x\right]_0^1$

$= \dfrac{1}{4} - \dfrac{7}{3} + \dfrac{15}{2} - 9 = \dfrac{3 - 28 + 90 - 108}{12}$

$= -\dfrac{43}{12} = -3\dfrac{7}{12}$

$= 3\dfrac{7}{12}$ s.u. (the negative sign indicate that the area is under the x-axis.)

(ii) $\int_1^3 (x^3 - 7x^2 + 15x - 9) dx$

$= \left[\dfrac{x^4}{4} - \dfrac{7}{3}x^3 + \dfrac{15}{2}x^2 - 9x\right]_1^3$

$= \left[\dfrac{81}{4} - \dfrac{7}{3}(27) + \dfrac{15}{2}(9) - 27\right] - \left(-3\dfrac{7}{12}\right)$

$= \dfrac{243 - 756 + 810 - 324}{12} + \dfrac{43}{12} = \dfrac{-27}{12} + \dfrac{43}{12} = \dfrac{16}{12}$

$= 1\dfrac{1}{4}$ s.u.

TOTAL FOR PAPER: 75 MARKS

GCE Examinations
Advanced Subsidiary

Test Paper 4

Core Mathematics C2
Time: 1 hour 30 minutes

Instructions and Information

Candidates are allowed to use calculators for this paper.

Full marks are awarded for answers to ALL questions.

This paper has ten questions.

You can start working with any question and you must label clearly all parts.

1. Show that, if $f(x)$ is divided by $(ax+b)$ the remainder is $f\left(-\frac{b}{a}\right)$, hence factorise $2x^2 + x - 1$. **(5)**

2.

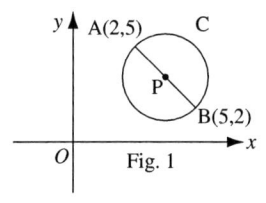

Fig. 1

Fig. 1 shows the coordinates of the end points of the diameter of a circle C.
Find
   (a) the exact length of the diameter, AB **(2)**
   (b) the coordinates of the centre P. **(2)**
   (c) the equation of the circle C in the form
       (i) $(x-a)^2 + (y-b)^2 = r^2$. **(3)**
       (ii) $x^2 + 2fx + 2gy + y^2 + c = 0$. **(3)**

---

3. The first term of a geometric series is 100. The sum to infinity of the series is 125.
   (a) Find the common ratio. **(3)**
   (b) Find, to 3d.p., the difference between the 10th and 11th terms. **(2)**
   (c) Calculate the sum of the first 10 terms. **(2)**

   The sum of the first n terms of the series is greater than 120.
   (d) Calculate the smallest possible value of n.

---

4. Expand $(a+b)^{10}$ and simplify. **(6)**

5. Fig. 2 shows a scalene triangle ABC.

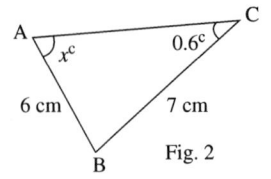

Fig. 2

$C\hat{A}B = x^c$
$C\hat{A}B = x$ radians.
$A\hat{C}B = 0.6^c$.
Determine:
(a) The value of x^c
(b) the value of B^c. (8)

6. (a) Solve $\cos(x + 30°) = \frac{\sqrt{3}}{2}$ for $-180° < x < 180°$. (2)

(b) Solve $6\cos^2 x° + \sin x° - 5 = 0$.
for $0 \leq x < 360$. (4)

(c) Solve $\sin\left(x + \frac{\pi}{4}\right) = \frac{\sqrt{3}}{2}$ for $0 < x < 2\pi$ (4)

7. (a) Show that $\log_a N = \frac{\log_b N}{\log_b a}$ (3)

hence find the values
(i) $\log_2 10$ (ii) $\log_3 20$, to 3 s.f. (2)

(b) Show that $\log_a b = \frac{1}{\log_b a}$. (3)

8. Explain the meaning of the second order derivative $\frac{d^2 y}{dx^2} = f''(x)$, illustrating your answer with the two parabolas as shown in Fig. 3.

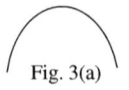

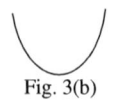

Fig. 3(a)   Fig. 3(b)

(6)

9. A curve is given by the cubic equation $y = (x-3)^3 = f(x)$
   Find (i) $f'(x)$
   (ii) $f''(x)$ (4)
   Explain the stationary points for the curve and state the set of values for increasing and decreasing function.
   Sketch the curve. (4)

10. Fig. 4 shows a parabola with equation $y = f(x) = -x^2 + 5$ and a straight line $y = \sqrt{5}x + 5$.

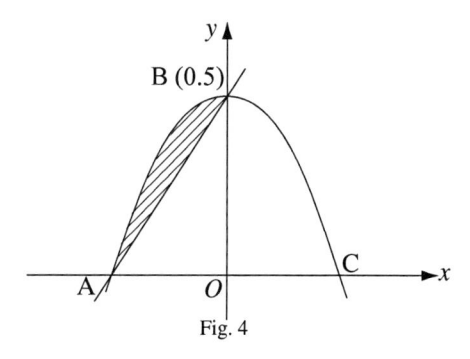

   Fig. 4

   Find
   (a) The coordinates of A, B and C. (3)
   (b) The exact value of the shaded area. (7)

TOTAL FOR PAPER: 75 MARKS

GCE Examinations
Advanced Subsidiary

Test Paper 4 Solutions

Core Mathematics C2
Time: 1 hour 30 minutes

Instructions and Information

Candidates are allowed to use calculators for this paper.

Full marks are awarded for answers to ALL questions.

This paper has ten questions.

You can start working with any question and you must label clearly all parts.

1. $\frac{f(x)}{ax+b} = Q(x) + \frac{R}{ax+b}$
   $f(x) = Q(x)(ax+b) + R$
   if $x = -\frac{b}{a}$
   $f\left(-\frac{b}{a}\right) = Q\left(-\frac{b}{a}\right)\left(a\left(-\frac{b}{a}\right)+b\right) + R$
   $\therefore f\left(-\frac{b}{a}\right) = R$
   $f(x) = 2x^2 + x - 1$
   $f\left(\frac{1}{2}\right) = 2\left(\frac{1}{4}\right) + \frac{1}{2} - 1 = 0$
   $\therefore 2x - 1$ is a factor

   $$\begin{array}{r} x + 1 \\ 2x-1 \overline{\smash{\big)}\, 2x^2 + x - 1} \\ \underline{2x^2 - x } \\ 2x - 1 \\ \underline{2x - 1} \\ 0 \end{array}$$

2. (a) $AB = \sqrt{(2-5)^2 + (5-2)^2} = \sqrt{3^2 + 3^2} = \sqrt{18}$ = diameter
   $= 3\sqrt{2}$.
   (b) $P\left(\frac{5+2}{2}, \frac{2+5}{2}\right) \equiv P\left(\frac{7}{2}, \frac{7}{2}\right)$.
   (c) (i) $\left(x - \frac{7}{2}\right)^2 + \left(y - \frac{7}{2}\right)^2 = \left(\frac{3\sqrt{2}}{2}\right)^2 = \frac{9}{2}$

   (ii) $x^2 - 7x + \frac{49}{4} + y^2 - 7y = \frac{9}{2} = 0$
   $x^2 - 7x + y^2 - 7y + 20 = 0$

3. (a) $S_\infty = \frac{a}{1-r} = \frac{100}{1-r} = 125$
   $1 - r = \frac{100}{125}$
   $1 - \frac{100}{125} = r = \frac{25}{125} = \frac{1}{5}$.

(b) $T_{10} - T_{11} = ar^9 - ar^{10}$
$$= 100\left(\tfrac{1}{5}\right)^9 - 100\left(\tfrac{1}{5}\right)^{10}$$
$$= 5.12 \times 10^{-5} - 1.024 \times 10^{-5}$$
$$= 4.096 \times 10^{-5}$$

(c) $S_{10} = 100\left[1 - \left(\tfrac{1}{5}\right)^{10}\right] \div \left(1 - \tfrac{1}{5}\right)$
$$= 99.99998976 \div 0.8$$
$$= 124.9999 = 125$$

(d) $S_n = \dfrac{100}{\left(1-\tfrac{1}{5}\right)}\left(1 - \left(\tfrac{1}{5}\right)^n\right] = 125 - 125\left(\tfrac{1}{5}\right)^n > 120$

$125 - 120 > \dfrac{125}{5^n}$

$5 > \dfrac{125}{5^n}$

$5^{n+1} > 125$

$\boxed{n = 3}$

---

4. $(a+b)^{10} = a^{10} + 10a^9b + \dfrac{10\times 9}{1\times 2}a^8b^2 + \dfrac{10\times 9\times 8}{1\times 2\times 3}a^7b^3$

$+ \dfrac{10\times 9\times 8\times 7}{1\times 2\times 3\times 4}a^6b^4 + \dfrac{10\times 9\times 8\times 7\times 6}{1\times 2\times 3\times 4\times 5}a^5b^5$

$+ \dfrac{10\times 9\times 8\times 7\times 6\times 5}{1\times 2\times 3\times 4\times 5\times 6}a^4b^6 + \dfrac{10\times 9\times 8\times 7\times 6\times 5\times 4}{1\times 2\times 3\times 4\times 5\times 6\times 7}a^3b^7$

$+ \dfrac{10\times 9\times 8\times 7\times 6\times 5\times 4\times 3}{1\times 2\times 3\times 4\times 5\times 6\times 7}a^2b^8 + \dfrac{10\times 9\times 8\times 7\times 6\times 5\times 4\times 3\times 2}{1\times 2\times 3\times 4\times 5\times 6\times 7\times 8}ab^9$

$+ b^{10}$

$= a^{10} + 10a^9b + 45a^8b^2 + 120a^7b^3 + 210a^6b^4$

$+ 252a^5b^5 + 210a^4b^6 + 120a^3b^7 + 45a^2b^8$

$+ 10ab^9 + b^{10}.$

5. (a) Using the sine rule
$$\frac{7}{\sin x^c} = \frac{6}{\sin 0.6^c} \qquad \text{Note: } x^c = \left(\frac{x180}{\pi}\right)^\circ$$
$$\sin x^c = \frac{7\sin 0.6^c}{6} = \frac{7\sin 34.37746771^\circ}{6}$$
$$= 0.658749552$$
$$x = \frac{41.20457613^\circ \times \pi}{180}$$
$$= 0.71915552^c$$

(b) $A^c + B^c + C^c = \pi$.
$$B^c = \pi - 0.71915552^c - 0.6^c$$
$$= 1.82^c.$$
$$B = 1.82^c.$$

6. (a) $\cos(x + 30^\circ) = \frac{\sqrt{3}}{2} = \cos 30^\circ = \cos 330^\circ$
$$x = 30^\circ - 30^\circ = \boxed{0^\circ}$$
$x = 300^\circ$ not valid for the range given.

(b) $6\cos^2 x^0 + \sin x^0 - 5 = 0$
$$\sin^2 x^0 + \cos^2 x = 1$$
$$\cos^2 x = 1 - \sin^2 x^0$$
$$6(1 - \sin^2 x^0) + \sin x^0 - 5 = 0$$
$$6 - 6\sin^2 x^0 + \sin x^0 - 5 = 0$$
$$6\sin^2 x^0 - \sin x^0 - 1 = 0$$
$$\sin x^0 = \frac{1 \pm \sqrt{1+24}}{12}$$
$$= \frac{1 \pm 5}{12}$$
$\sin x^0 = \frac{1}{2}$ or $\sin x^0 = -\frac{1}{3}$
$\sin x^0 = \sin 30^\circ = \sin 150^\circ$
$$x = 30 \text{ or } 150$$
$\sin x^0 = -\frac{1}{3}$ is not valid for the range given.

(c) $\sin\left(x + \frac{\pi}{4}\right) = \sin\frac{\pi}{3} = \sin\frac{2\pi}{3}$

$x + \frac{\pi}{4} = \frac{\pi}{3} \Rightarrow x = \frac{\pi}{12}$

$x + \frac{\pi}{4} = \frac{2\pi}{3} \Rightarrow x = \frac{5\pi}{12}$.

---

7. (a) To show $\log_a N = \frac{\log_b N}{\log_b a}$

let $y = \log_a N$

by definition $N = a^y$

taking logarithms to the base b

$\log_b N = \log_b a^y$

$= y \log_b a$

$y = \frac{\log_b N}{\log_b a}$

$\therefore \log_a N = \frac{\log_b N}{\log_b a}$

$\log_2 10 = \frac{\log_{10} 10}{\log_{10} 2} = \frac{1}{0.301029995} = 3.32$ to 3 s.f.

$\log_3 20 = \frac{\log_{10} 20}{\log_{10} 3} = 2.726833078$

$= 2.73$ to 3 s.f.

(b) $\log_a b = \frac{\log_b b}{\log_b a} = \frac{1}{\log_b a}$.

---

8. $\frac{d^2y}{dx^2} = \frac{d}{dx}\left(\frac{dy}{dx}\right) =$ the rate of change of the gradient $\left(\frac{dy}{dx}\right)$

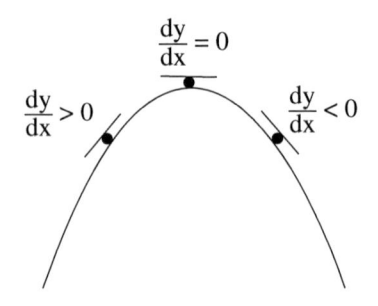

The gradient changes from positive to negative via $\frac{dy}{dx} = 0$

$\therefore \frac{d}{dx}\left(\frac{dy}{dx}\right) = \frac{d^2y}{dx^2} < 0$

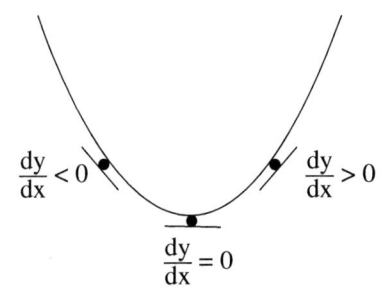

$\frac{dy}{dx} < 0 \qquad \frac{dy}{dx} > 0$

$\frac{dy}{dx} = 0$

The gradient changes from negative to positive via $\frac{dy}{dx} = 0$

$\therefore \frac{d}{dx}\left(\frac{dx}{dy}\right) = \frac{d^2y}{dx^2} > 0.$

9.

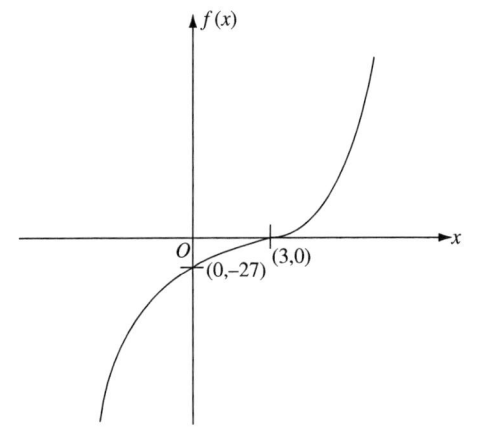

$f(x) = (x-3)^3$
$f'(x) = 3(x-3)^2$
$f''(x) = 6(x-3)$
$f'(x) = 0$ for stationary values
$3(x-3)^2 = 0$
$x = 3$ twice

Graph passes through $(0, -27)$ and $(3, 0)$.

$f''(3) = 6(3-3) = 0$
The second order derivative is neither positive nor negative, it is zero $\frac{d^2y}{dx^2} = 0$, point of inflection. The gradient is always positive.

10. (a) $y = -x^2 + 5 = f(x)$
$f(0) = 5$
$\therefore B(0, 5)$
$f(x) = 0 = -x^2 + 5$
$x^2 = 5$
$x = \pm\sqrt{5}$
$A(-\sqrt{5}, 0), C(\sqrt{5}, 0)$

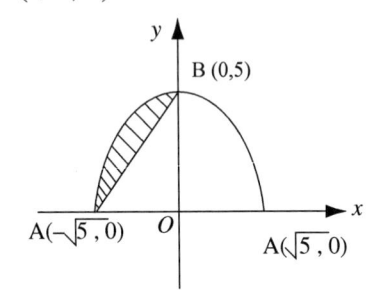

(b) The area between the curve and the axes.
$$\int_{-\sqrt{5}}^{0}(-x^2 + 5)dx = \left[\frac{-x^3}{3} + 5x\right]_{-\sqrt{5}}^{0}$$
$$= -\left[-\frac{(-\sqrt{5})^3}{3} + 5(-\sqrt{5})\right]$$
$$= \frac{-5\sqrt{5}}{3} + 5\sqrt{5}$$
$$= \frac{-5\sqrt{5} + 15\sqrt{5}}{3} = \frac{10\sqrt{5}}{3} \text{s.u.}$$

The area of the triangle ABO
$$= \frac{OA \times OB}{2} = \frac{\sqrt{5} \times 5}{2}$$
$$= \frac{5}{2}\sqrt{5}$$

shaded area $= \frac{10}{3}\sqrt{5} - \frac{5}{2}\sqrt{5}$
$$= \frac{20\sqrt{5} - 15\sqrt{5}}{6}$$
$$= \frac{5}{6}\sqrt{5} \text{ s.u.}$$

TOTAL FOR PAPER: 75 MARKS

GCE Examinations
Advanced Subsidiary

Test Paper 5

Core Mathematics C2
Time: 1 hour 30 minutes

Instructions and Information

Candidates are allowed to use calculators for this paper.

Full marks are awarded for answers to ALL questions.

This paper has ten questions.

You can start working with any question and you must label clearly all parts.

1. Solve the cubic equation $f(x) = x^3 - 3x + 2$. (4)

2. The circle C, with centre at the point P, has equation
   $x^2 - 8x + y^2 - 10y + 5 = 0$.

   Find (i) the coordinates of P, (2)

   (ii) the radius of C, (2)

   (iii) the exact coordinates of the points at which C crosses the x-axis. (2)

3. (a) The first term of a geometric series is 162 and the common ratio is $\frac{1}{3}$ find the sum of the first 4 terms. (3)

   (b) Find the sum to infinity of a geometric series where $a = 81$ and $r = \frac{1}{3}$. (2)

   (c) If $S_\infty - S_n > 0.0001$, determine n, for (a). (5)

4. (a) Find the first 3 terms in ascending powers of x, of the binomial expansion
   $$(1 + px)^{11},$$
   where p is a constant. (2)

   The first 3 terms are $1, qx, 220x^2$ where q is a constant.

   (b) Find the values of p and the values q. (4)

5. Fig. 1 shows a sector of *ABC* of a circle, of radius 15 cm. The chord *AB* is 20 cm long.

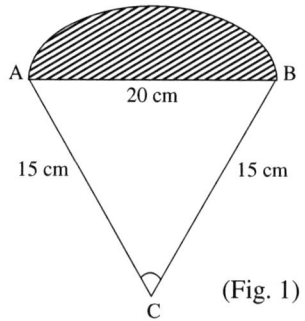

(Fig. 1)

(a) Show that $\cos A\hat{C}B = \frac{1}{12}$. **(2)**

(b) Hence find the angle $A\hat{C}B$ in radians, giving your answer to 3 significant figures. **(1)**

(c) Calculate the area of the $\triangle ABC$ **(2)**

(d) Hence calculate the shaded area. **(3)**

---

6. Sketch the graphs:
   (a) $f(x) = \sin x$ **(2)**
   (b) $3f(x)$ **(2)**
   (c) $f\left(x - \frac{\pi}{6}\right)$ **(2)**
   (d) $f(2x)$ **(2)**

   for $-2\pi \leq x \leq 2\pi$.

---

7. (a) Evaluate $5 \log 64 - \log 36 - 3 \log\left(\frac{1}{8}\right) + 3 \log 100$ to 3 s.f. by first applying the rules of logarithms, giving your answer to 3 s.f. **(3)**

   (b) Solve the equation
   $$5^{x+3} + 5^{x+1} = 100$$
   giving your answer to 3 d.p. **(5)**

8. A right circular cylinder is to be cut from a right circular solid cone as shown in Fig. 2. If x is the radius of the cylinder find an expression for the volume, V, of the cylinder in terms of x, r and h, **(3)**

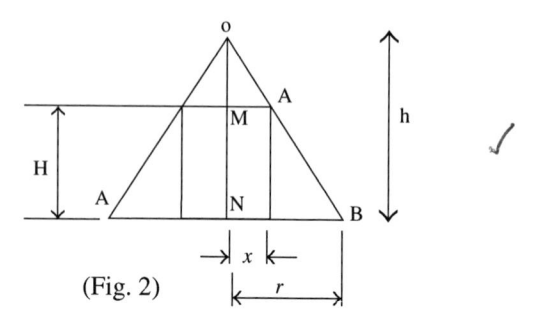

(Fig. 2)

hence find the maximum volume of the cylinder as x varies, if $r = 3$ m and $h = \frac{3}{4\pi}$ m. **(9)**

9.

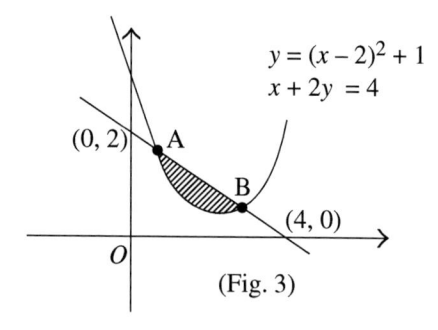

(Fig. 3)

Fig. 3 shows the equation of the curve and the equation of a line.

(a) Determine the coordinates of A and B **(3)**

(b) Determine the exact shaded area. **(6)**

10. A curve whose equation is $y = f(x)$ passes through the points defined in the following table

x	0.1	0.2	0.3	0.4	0.5	0.6
y	25	29.6	35.9	42	46	52

✓

use the trapezoital rule with six ordinates to evaluate $\int_{0.1}^{0.6} y \, dx$. **(4)**

TOTAL FOR PAPER: 75 MARKS

GCE Examinations
Advanced Subsidiary

Test Paper 5 Solutions

Core Mathematics C2
Time: 1 hour 30 minutes

Instructions and Information

Candidates are allowed to use calculators for this paper.

Full marks are awarded for answers to ALL questions.

This paper has ten questions.

You can start working with any question and you must label clearly all parts.

1. $f(x) = x^3 - 3x + 2$
   $f(-2) = -8 + 6 + 2 = 0$
   $\therefore x + 2$ is a factor

   $$\begin{array}{r}
   x^2 - 2x + 1 \\
   x+2 \overline{\smash{\big)} x^3 - 3x + 2} \\
   \underline{x^3 + 2x^2} \\
   -2x^2 - 3x + 2 \\
   \underline{-2x^2 - 4x} \\
   x + 2 \\
   \underline{x + 2} \\
   0
   \end{array}$$

   $\therefore f(x) = (x+2)(x^2 - 2x + 1)$
   $\quad = (x+2)(x-1)^2$
   $f(x) = 0$
   $\quad (x+2)(x-1)^2 = 0$
   $\quad x = -2,$ or $x = 1$ twice.

---

2. $x^2 - 8x + y^2 - 10y + 5 = 0$
   $(x-4)^2 - 16 + (y-5)^2 - 25 + 5 = 0$
   $(x-4)^2 + (y-5)^2 = 6^2$.
   (i) $P(4, 5)$
   (ii) $r = 6$
   (iii) when $y = 0$, $(x-4)^2 = 36 - 25$
   $\qquad\qquad\qquad\qquad = 11$
   $\qquad\qquad\therefore x = 4 \pm \sqrt{11}$
   $(4 - \sqrt{11}, 0)$ and $(4 + \sqrt{11}, 0)$.

3. (a) $a = 162, r = \frac{1}{3}$

$$S_4 = \frac{162}{1-\frac{1}{3}}\left[1 - \left(\frac{1}{3}\right)^4\right] = \frac{162}{\frac{2}{3}}\left[1 - \frac{1}{81}\right]$$
$$= \frac{81 \times 3 \times 80}{81}$$
$$= 240.$$

(b) $S_\infty = \frac{a}{1-r} = \frac{81}{\frac{2}{3}} = \frac{243}{2} = 121.5$

(c) $S_\infty = 243$

$S_n = 243\left[1 - \left(\frac{1}{3}\right)^n\right]$

$243 - 243\left[1 - \frac{1}{3^n}\right] = \frac{243}{3^n} > 0.0001$

$\frac{3^5}{3^n} > 0.0001 \Rightarrow 3^{5-n} > 0.0001 = \frac{1}{10000}$

Alternatively taking logarithms to the base 10 of (1)

$(n - 5)\log 3 < \log 10000$

$n - 5 < \frac{\log 10000}{\log 3}$

$n - 5 < 8.383613097$

$n < 13.383613097$

$n = 13.$

4. $(1+px)^{11} = 1 + 11px + \frac{11 \times 10}{1 \times 2} p^2 x^2$.

Equating coefficients of x and x^2

$$11p = q$$
$$55p^2 = 220$$
$$p = \pm 2$$
$$q = 11(\pm 2) = \pm 22.$$

---

5. (a)

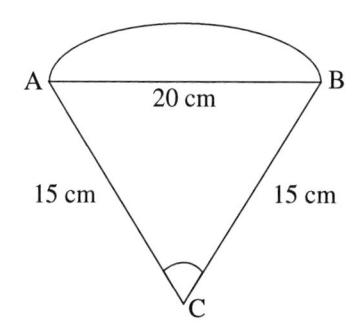

using the cosine rule
$$AB^2 = AC^2 + BC^2 - 2 \times AB \times BC \cos A\hat{C}B$$
$$2 \times 20 \times 15 \cos A\hat{C}B = 15^2 + 15^2 - 20^2$$
$$\cos A\hat{C}B = \frac{225 + 225 - 400}{2 \times 20 \times 15}$$
$$= \frac{50}{600} = \frac{1}{12}.$$

(b) $\cos A\hat{C}B = \frac{1}{12}$

$$A\hat{C}B = 1.48736684^c$$
$$= 1.49^c \text{ to 3 s.f.}$$

(c) Area $\triangle ABC = \frac{1}{2} \times 15 \times 15 \sin A\hat{C}B$
$$= \frac{1}{2} \times 225 \times 0.996521728$$
$$= \frac{1}{2} \times 224.2173889$$
$$= 112 \text{ cm}^2 \text{ to 3 s.f.}$$

(d) shaded area = Area of sector ABC - area $\triangle ABC$
$$= \tfrac{1}{2}15^2 \times 1.48736624 - 112.108695$$
$$= 55.220007$$
$$= 55.2 \text{cm}^2 \text{ to 3 s.f.}$$

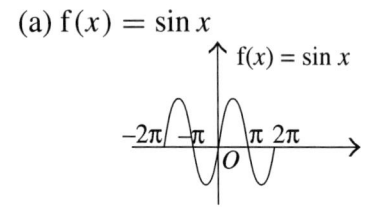

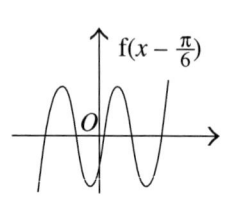

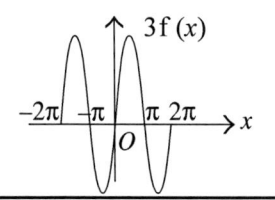

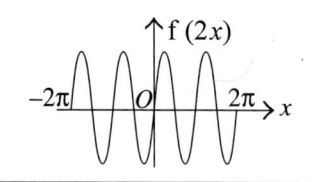

6. (a) $f(x) = \sin x$

(c) $f(x - \tfrac{\pi}{6})$

(b) $3f(x)$

(d) $f(2x)$

7. (a) $5\log 64 - \log 36 - 3\log\left(\tfrac{1}{8}\right) + 3\log 100$
$$= \log 64^5 - \log 36 - \log\left(\tfrac{1}{2^3}\right)^3 + \log 100^3$$
$$= \log \tfrac{64^5}{36} \times 2^9 \times 100^3 = 16.2 \text{ to 3 s.f.}$$

(b) $5^{x+3} + 5^{x+1} = 100$
$$5^{x+1}5^2 + 5^{x+1} = 100 = 0$$
$$25(5^{x+1}) + 5^{x+1} = 100$$
$$26(5^{x+1}) = 100$$
$$5^{x+1} = \tfrac{100}{26}$$
$$x + 1 = \tfrac{\log \tfrac{100}{26}}{\log 5} = \tfrac{0.585026652}{0.698970004}$$
$$= 0.836983916$$
$$x = -0.163016083 = -0.163.$$

8. $V = \pi x^2 H$ the volume of the cylinder consider the right angled triangles, OMA and ONB
$$\frac{AM}{NB} = \frac{x}{r} = \frac{h-H}{h} = 1 - \frac{H}{h} \Rightarrow \frac{H}{h} = 1 - \frac{x}{r} \Rightarrow H = h\left(1 - \frac{x}{r}\right)$$
$$V = \pi x^2 h \left(1 - \frac{x}{r}\right) = \pi x^2 h - \frac{\pi h x^3}{r}$$
differentiating V with respect to x
$$\frac{dV}{dx} = 2\pi x h - \frac{\pi h}{r} 3 x^2$$
$\frac{dV}{dx} = 0$ for turning points
$$2\pi x h - \frac{3\pi h x^2}{r} = 0$$
$$2\pi x h = \frac{3\pi h x^2}{r}$$
$$x = \frac{2r}{3}$$
$$\frac{d^2 V}{dx^2} = 2\pi h - \frac{6\pi h}{r} x = 2\pi h - \frac{6\pi h}{r} \frac{2r}{3}$$
$$= -2h\pi < 0 \quad \therefore \text{maximum}$$
$$V_{max} = \pi \frac{4r^2}{9} h \left(1 - \frac{2r}{3r}\right)$$
$$V_{max} = \frac{4\pi r^2 h}{27} = \frac{4\pi}{27}(3)^2 \left(\frac{3}{4\pi}\right) = 1 \text{m}^3.$$

9. (a) $(x - 2)^2 + 1 = y \quad \ldots (1)$
$\qquad x + 2y = 4 \quad \ldots (2)$ substituting y in (1)
$\qquad (x - 2)^2 + 1 = \frac{4-x}{2}$
$\qquad 2(x^2 - 4x + 4) + 2 = 4 - x$
$\qquad 2x^2 - 8x + 8 + 2 - 4 + x = 0$
$\qquad 2x^2 - 7x + 6 = 0$
$\qquad (2x - 3)(x - 2) = 0$
$\qquad x = 2, \text{ or } x = \frac{3}{2}$
$\qquad$ when $x = 2, y = 1$
$\qquad$ when $x = \frac{3}{2}, y = \frac{5}{4}$.
$\qquad \therefore A\left(\frac{3}{2}, \frac{5}{4}\right), B(2, 1).$

(b) Area under the curve

$$\int_{\frac{3}{2}}^{2} [(x-2)^2 + 1]\,dx = \left[\frac{(x-2)^3}{3} + x\right]_{\frac{3}{2}}^{2}$$

$$= 2 - \left[\frac{\left(-\frac{1}{2}\right)^3}{3} + \frac{3}{2}\right]$$

$$= 2 + \frac{1}{24} - \frac{3}{2}$$

$$= 2 + \frac{1}{24}$$

$$= \frac{13}{24}.$$

Area of trapezium

$$= \frac{1}{2}\left(\frac{5}{4} + 1\right) \times \frac{1}{2} = \frac{9}{4} \times \frac{1}{4} = \frac{9}{16}$$

shaded area $= \frac{9}{16} - \frac{13}{24}$

$$= \frac{1}{8}\left(\frac{9}{2} - \frac{13}{3}\right)$$

$$= \frac{1}{8} \times \frac{27-26}{6}$$

$$= \frac{1}{48} \text{ s.u.}$$

---

10. $\int_{0.1}^{0.6} y\,dx \approx \frac{h}{2}[y_0 + 2(y_1 + y_2 + y_3 + y_4) + y_5]$

$$= \frac{0.1}{2}[25 + 2(29.6 + 35.9 + 42 + 46) + 52]$$

$$= 0.05(77 + 2 \times 153.5)$$

$$= 0.05 \times 384$$

$$= 19.2 \text{ s.u.}$$

TOTAL FOR PAPER: 75 MARKS

GCE Examinations
Advanced Subsidiary

Test Paper 6

Core Mathematics C2
Time: 1 hour 30 minutes

Instructions and Information

Candidates are allowed to use calculators for this paper.

Full marks are awarded for answers to ALL questions.

This paper has ten questions.

You can start working with any question and you must label clearly all parts.

1. Solve the cubic equation
$$f(x) = 2x^3 + 11x^2 + 12x - 9 = 0.$$ **(5)**

---

2. Fig. 1 shows the curve of a circle

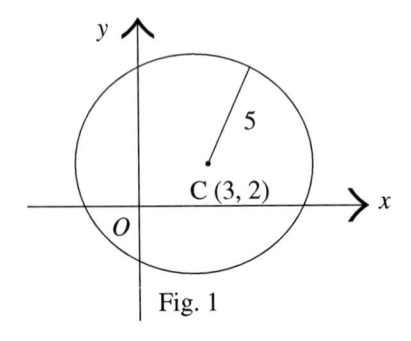

Fig. 1

Find: (a) the equation of the circle **(3)**

(b) the exact coordinates of the points of intersections with the exes. **(6)**

---

3. All the terms of a certain geometric series are positive. The first term is p and the second term is $p^2 - 2p$.

Find the set of values of p for which the series converges. **(4)**

---

4. Expand $(3 - 4x)^5$, simplify the expression. **(4)**

5.

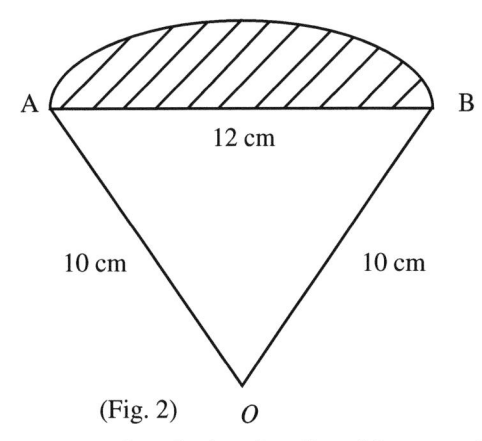

Fig. 2 shows a sector of a circle of radius 10 cm and a chord $AB = 12$ cm

Determine: (a) The cosine of the angle AÔB. **(2)**

(b) The angle AÔB in radians. **(1)**

(c) The area of the sector AOB. **(2)**

(d) The shaded area. **(3)**

---

6. Solve the equation
$$\sin^2\left(x - \tfrac{\pi}{4}\right) = \tfrac{1}{2}$$
for $-\pi < x < \pi$. **(8)**

---

7. Find the values of x which satisfy the equation
$$2^{3x} - 6 \times 2^{2x+1} + 41 \times 2^x = 30$$ **(10)**

8. Fig. 3 shows an arc of length s subtended by an angle θ (radians), the radius of the circle is r.

   The length of the arc is given by $s = r\theta$.
   The area of the triangle ABO $\Delta_1 = \frac{1}{2}r^2 \sin\theta$.
   The area of the sector ABO is $\Delta_2 = \frac{1}{2}r^2\theta$.
   Express the area of the triangle and sector in terms of s. (2)

   Find the maximum area of the triangle Δ_1 assuming r is constant and s is variable. Verify that the area is maximum. (4)

   What is the area of the sector Δ_2, for this condition? (2)

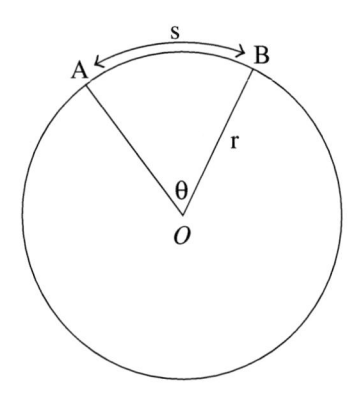

9. (a) Sketch the curves:

   (i) $y = 3x^2$ and (ii) $y = 5 - x^2$.

   show that the coordinates of the points of intersection of (i) and (ii) are:
   $$A\left(-\frac{\sqrt{5}}{2}, \frac{15}{4}\right) \text{ and } B\left(\frac{\sqrt{5}}{2}, \frac{15}{4}\right).$$ (4)

   (b) Determine exactly the area of the curve (1), the x-axis and the lines
   $$x = -\frac{\sqrt{5}}{2} \text{ and } x = \frac{\sqrt{5}}{2}.$$ (4)

10. A curve whose equation is $y = f(x)$ passes through the points defined in the table:

x	1	2	3	4	5	6	7	8	9
y	5	9	12	16	19	23	26	30	33

Use the trapezoidal rule with nine ordinates to evaluate $\int_1^9 f(x)\,dx$. **(8)**

and hence determine approximately the average ordinate in the range $1 \leq x \leq 9$. **(3)**

TOTAL FOR PAPER: 75 MARKS

GCE Examinations
Advanced Subsidiary

Test Paper 6 Solutions

Core Mathematics C2
Time: 1 hour 30 minutes

Instructions and Information

Candidates are allowed to use calculators for this paper.

Full marks are awarded for answers to ALL questions.

This paper has ten questions.

You can start working with any question and you must label clearly all parts.

1. $f(x) = 2x^3 + 11x^2 + 12x - 9$ let $x = \frac{1}{2}$

$f\left(\frac{1}{2}\right) = 2\left(\frac{1}{8}\right) + 11\left(\frac{1}{4}\right) + 12\left(\frac{1}{2}\right) - 9$

$\phantom{f\left(\frac{1}{2}\right)} = \frac{1}{4} + \frac{11}{4} + 6 - 9$

$\phantom{f\left(\frac{1}{2}\right)} = 0$

$\therefore 2x - 1$ is a factor

$$\begin{array}{r}
x^2 + 6x + 9 \\
2x - 1 \overline{\smash{)}\, 2x^3 + 11x^2 + 12x - 9} \\
\underline{2x^3 - x^2} \\
12x^2 + 12x - 9 \\
\underline{12x^2 - 6x} \\
18x - 9 \\
\underline{18x - 9} \\
0
\end{array}$$

$\therefore f(x) = (2x - 1)(x^2 + 6x + 9)$
$ = (2x - 1)(x + 3)^2$

$f(x) = 0$
$(2x - 1) = 0 \Rightarrow x = \frac{1}{2}$
$(x + 3)^2 = 0 \Rightarrow x = -3$ twice.

2.

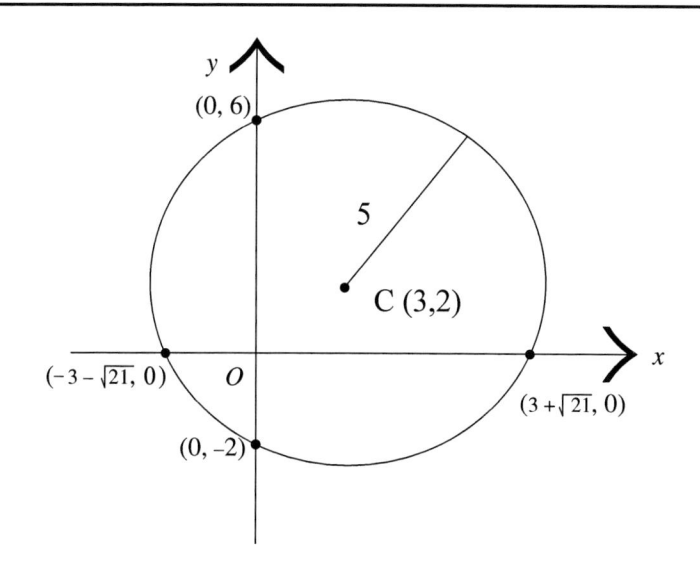

(a) $(x-3)^2 + (y-2)^2 = 5^2$

(b) $(x-3)^2 = 25 - 4 = 21$, $y = 0$

$x = 3 \pm \sqrt{21}$

$(-3)^2 + (y-2)^2 = 5^2 \Rightarrow y = 2 \pm 4$, $x = 0$.

---

3. $p, p^2 - 2p, \ldots$ $r = \frac{p^2 - 2p}{p}$

$\left|\frac{p^2 - 2p}{p}\right| < 1$ for convergence

$p^2 - 2p < p$

$p^2 - 3p < 0$

$p(p-3) < 0$

$0 < p < 3$.

---

4. $(3 - 4x)^5 = 3^5 + 5 \times 3^4(-4x) + \frac{5 \times 4}{1 \times 2} \times 3^3(-4x)^2$

$+ \frac{5 \times 4 \times 3}{1 \times 2 \times 3} \times 3^2(-4x)^3 + \frac{5 \times 4 \times 3 \times 2}{1 \times 2 \times 3 \times 4} \times 3 \times (-4x)^4$

$+ (-4x)^5$

$= 243 - 1620x + 4320x^2 - 5760x^3$

$+ 3840x^4 - 1024x^5$.

---

5. (a) Using the cosine rule for the $\triangle ABO$

$12^2 = 10^2 + 10^2 - 2 \times 10 \times 10 \cos A\hat{O}B$

$\cos A\hat{O}B = \frac{100 + 100 - 144}{2 \times 10 \times 10} = \frac{56}{200}$

$= \frac{14}{50} = \frac{7}{25}$.

(b) $A\hat{O}B = 1.287002218^c = 1.29^c$ to 3s.f.

(c) $\frac{1}{2} \times 10 \times 10 \times 1.287002718^c = 64.3501109 = 64.4 \text{cm}^2$ 3 s.f.

(d) shaded area $= 64.3501109 - \frac{1}{2} 10 \times 10 \sin 1.287002218$

$= 16.3 \text{ cm}^2$ to 3.s.f.

6. $\sin^2\left(x - \frac{\pi}{4}\right) = \frac{1}{2}$

   square rooting both sides

   $\sin\left(x - \frac{\pi}{4}\right) = \pm\frac{1}{\sqrt{2}}$

   $\sin\left(x - \frac{\pi}{4}\right) = \frac{1}{\sqrt{2}} = \sin\frac{\pi}{4} = \sin\frac{3\pi}{4}$

   $x = \frac{\pi}{2}$ or $x = \pi$

   the only solution is $\boxed{x = \frac{\pi}{2}}$

   for the range given

   $\sin\left(x - \frac{\pi}{4}\right) = -\frac{1}{\sqrt{2}} = \sin\left(-\frac{\pi}{4}\right) = \sin\left(-\frac{3\pi}{4}\right)$

   $x = \frac{\pi}{4} - \frac{\pi}{4} = 0 \Rightarrow \boxed{x = 0}$

   $x = \frac{\pi}{4} - \frac{3\pi}{4} \Rightarrow \boxed{x = -\frac{\pi}{2}}$

   $\sin\left(x - \frac{\pi}{4}\right) = \sin\left(-\frac{9\pi}{4}\right)$

   $x - \frac{\pi}{4} = -\frac{9\pi}{4}$

   $\boxed{x = -2\pi}$ this is also not valid for the range given.

---

7. $\qquad 2^{3x} - 6 \times 2^{2x+1} + 41 \times 2^x = 30$

   $\qquad 2^{3x} - 6 \times 2^{2x} \times 2^1 + 41 \times 2^x - 30 = 0$ where $y = 2^x$

   $\qquad y^3 - 12y^2 + 41y - 30 = 0$

   $f(y) = y^3 - 12y^2 + 41y - 30$

   $f(1) = 1 - 12 + 41 - 30 = 0$

   $\therefore y - 1$ is a factor

$$
\begin{array}{r}
y^2 - 11y + 30 \\
y - 1 \overline{\smash{\big)}\, y^3 - 12y^2 + 41y - 30} \\
\underline{y^3 - y^2} \\
-11y^2 + 41y - 30 \\
\underline{-11y^2 + 11y} \\
30y - 30 \\
\underline{30y - 30} \\
0
\end{array}
$$

$$f(y) = (y-1)(y^2 - 11y + 30) = 0$$
$$(y-1)(y-5)(y-6) = 0$$
$$y = 1 \Rightarrow 2^x \Rightarrow x = 0$$
$$y = 5 \Rightarrow 2^x = 5 \Rightarrow x = \frac{\log 5}{\log 2}$$
$$= 2.32 \text{ to 3.s.f.}$$
$$y = 6 \Rightarrow 2^x = 6 \Rightarrow x = \frac{\log 6}{\log 2} = 2.58 \text{ to 3 s.f.}$$

---

8. $\Delta_1 = \frac{1}{2} r^2 \sin\theta = \frac{1}{2} r^2 \sin\left(\frac{s}{r}\right)$

$\frac{d\Delta_1}{ds} = 0$ for maximum area

$\frac{d\Delta_1}{ds} = \frac{1}{2} r^2 \left(\frac{1}{r}\right) \cos\left(\frac{s}{r}\right)$

$\phantom{\frac{d\Delta_1}{ds}} = \frac{1}{2} r \cos\left(\frac{s}{r}\right) = 0$ ...(1)

[chain rule is used here $\frac{d}{dx}(\sin kx) = k\cos kx$]

From (1)

$\cos\frac{s}{r} = 0 = \cos\frac{\pi}{2}$

$\therefore \frac{s}{r} = \frac{\pi}{2}$

$\frac{d^2 \Delta_1}{ds^2} = -\frac{1}{2} r^2 \left(\frac{1}{r}\right)\left(\frac{1}{r}\right) \sin\frac{s}{r}$

$\frac{d^2 \Delta_1}{ds^2} = -\frac{1}{2}\sin\frac{s}{r} = -\frac{1}{2}\sin r \frac{\pi}{2} \frac{1}{r} = -\frac{1}{2}\sin\frac{\pi}{2} = -\frac{1}{2} < 0$

(product rule is used here) which is in C_3

∴ maximum

$(\Delta_1)_{max} = \frac{1}{2}r^2 \sin\left(\frac{s}{r}\right) = \frac{1}{2}r^2 \sin\left(r\frac{\frac{\pi}{2}}{r}\right) = \frac{1}{2}r^2.$

$\Delta_2 = \frac{1}{2}r^2\theta = \frac{1}{2}r^2\frac{s}{r} = \frac{1}{2}rs = \frac{1}{2}rr\frac{\pi}{2} = \frac{r^2\pi}{4}.$

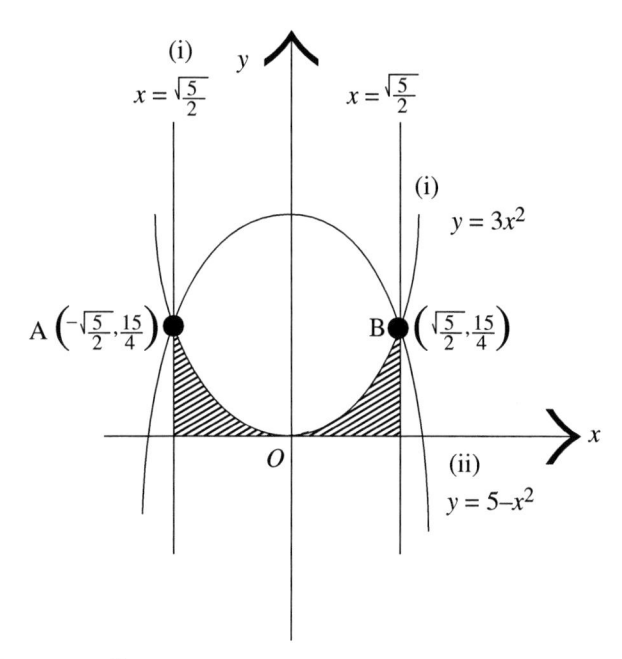

---

9. (a)

$3x^2 = 5 - x^2$
$4x^2 = 5$
$x^2 = \frac{5}{4} \Rightarrow x = \pm\frac{\sqrt{5}}{4}$
$x = -\frac{\sqrt{5}}{2}, y = \frac{15}{4}$

(b) $2\int_{-\frac{\sqrt{5}}{2}}^{0} 3x^2 dx = \left[2\left(\frac{3x^3}{3}\right)\right]_{-\frac{\sqrt{5}}{2}}^{0}$

$\qquad = 2\left(\frac{\sqrt{5}}{2}\right)\frac{5}{4}$

$\qquad = \frac{5\sqrt{5}}{4}$ s.u.

10. $\int_1^9 f(x)dx \approx \frac{1}{2}[5 + 33 + 2(9 + 12 + 16 + 19 + 23 + 26 + 30)]$
$= \frac{1}{2}(38 + 2 \times 135) = 154\text{s.u.}$
$\frac{154}{8} = 19.3$ to 3s.f.

TOTAL FOR PAPER: 75 MARKS

GCE Examinations
Advanced Subsidiary

Test Paper 7

Core Mathematics C2
Time: 1 hour 30 minutes

Instructions and Information

Candidates are allowed to use calculators for this paper.

Full marks are awarded for answers to ALL questions.

This paper has ten questions.

You can start working with any question and you must label clearly all parts.

1. (a) Divide $x+5$ by $x+1$. (2)
   (b) Divide $2x^2+x-3$ by $x-1$, hence factorise $2x^2+x-3$. (3)
   (c) Show that $x=-1$ is a solution of $f(x)=x^3+7x^2+15x+9$ hence solve $f(x)=0$. (5)

---

2. (a) The general equation of a circle is given $x^2+y^2-10x+6y-2=0$.
   Determine : (i) The coordinates of the centre of the circle.
   (ii) The radius. (5)
   (b) Sketch the circle, indicating the coordinates of the points of the intersections with the axes. (5)

---

3. (a) A convergent geometric series is given $\frac{1}{1}, \frac{1}{5}, \frac{1}{25}, \frac{1}{125}, \ldots$
   Determine : (i) The nth term of this series.
   (ii) The sum to infinity. (4)
   (b) Deduce (iii) The formula in (i) and (iv) prove the formula used in (ii). (5)

---

4. (a) Expand $(2+3x)^5 = a+bx+cx^2+dx^2+ex^4+fx^5$ and write down the simplified answers of a, b, c, d, e and f. (5)
   (b) Write down (n!) and $\binom{n}{r}$ hence show that 0! is unity, and $\binom{5}{3}=10$. (3)

5.

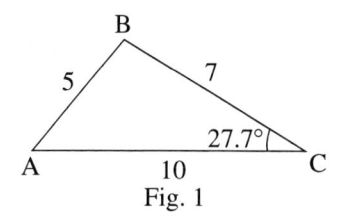

A scalene triangle is given in Fig. 1.

Use the cosine rule to find angle A and hence use the sine rule to find angles B and C and check yours answers. **(8)**

---

6. (a) Prove the formula
$$\log_a N = \frac{\log_b N}{\log_b a} \quad \textbf{(4)}$$

(b) Find the value of $\log_6 5$. **(1)**

(c) Sketch the graphs 2^x, e^x, 3^x, where $2 < e < 3$. **(3)**

---

7. Figure 2 shows the curve $y = \frac{1}{x^2}$ and the straight line $y = 1$ and $y = 3$.

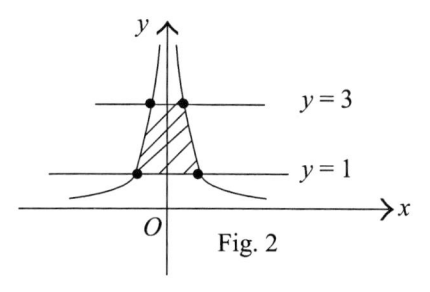

Show that the exact hatched area is $4(\sqrt{3} - 1)$. **(8)**

8. A cubic function is given

$f(x) = x^3 + 2x^2 - 5x - 6$.

Determine (i) $f'(x)$ and $f''(x)$. **(2)**

(ii) The coordinates of the turning points. **(3)**

Sketch the graph and insert the values found. **(3)**

9.

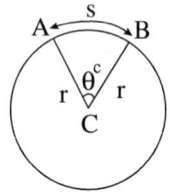

(i) Prove that the length of arc AB is $s = r\theta^c$. **(2)**

(ii) Prove that the area of the sector ABC is $\frac{1}{2}r^2\theta^c$. **(2)**

(iii) Write down the corresponding angles in degrees in terms of π.

$\theta°$ 0 30 45 60 90 120 135 150 180 210 225 240 270 300 315 330 360. **(2)**

TOTAL FOR PAPER: 75 MARKS

GCE Examinations
Advanced Subsidiary

Test Paper 7 Solutions

Core Mathematics C2
Time: 1 hour 30 minutes

Instructions and Information

Candidates are allowed to use calculators for this paper.

Full marks are awarded for answers to ALL questions.

This paper has ten questions.

You can start working with any question and you must label clearly all parts.

This paper may be reproduced in accordance with PASS PUBLICATIONS (Private Academic & Scientific Studies Limited)

1. (a) $\dfrac{x+5}{x+1} = 1 + \dfrac{4}{x+1}$

$$\begin{array}{r} 1 \\ x+1 \overline{\smash{)}\, x+5} \\ \underline{x+1} \\ 4 \end{array}$$

by long division, giving a quotient of 1 and the remainder of 4.

Alternatively

$$\dfrac{x+5}{x+1} = \dfrac{(x+1)+4}{x+1} = \dfrac{x+1}{x+1} + \dfrac{4}{x+1} = 1 + \dfrac{4}{x+1}.$$

(b) $\dfrac{2x^2 + x - 3}{x - 1} = 2x + 3$

$$\begin{array}{r} 2x+3 \\ x-1 \overline{\smash{)}\, 2x^2 + x - 3} \\ \underline{2x^2 - 2x} \\ 3x - 3 \\ \underline{3x - 3} \\ 0 \end{array}$$

$\therefore 2x^2 + x - 3 = (x-1)(2x+3)$.

(c) $f(x) = x^3 + 7x^2 + 15x + 9$

$f(-1) = (-1)^3 + 7(-1)^2 + 15(-1) + 9$

$ = -1 + 7 - 15 + 9 = 0$

$\therefore x + 1$ is a factor of $f(x)$

$$\begin{array}{r} x^2 + 6x + 9 \\ x+1 \overline{\smash{)}\, x^3 + 7x^2 + 15x + 9} \\ \underline{x^3 + x^2} \\ 6x^2 + 15x + 9 \\ \underline{6x^2 + 6x} \\ 9x + 9 \\ \underline{9x + 9} \\ 0 \end{array}$$

$\therefore f(x) = (x^2 + 6x + 9)(x + 1) = 0$
$= (x + 3)^2(x + 1) = 0$
$x = -3$ (twice) and $x = -1$.

---

2. (a) $x^2 + y^2 - 10x + 6y - 2 = 0$.

    Using the method of completing the square
    $[x^2 - 10x] + [y^2 + 6y] - 2 = 0$
    $[(x - 5)^2 - 25] + [(y + 3)^2 - 9] - 2 = 0$
    $(x - 5)^2 - 25 + (y + 3)^2 - 9 - 2 = 0$
    $(x - 5)^2 + (y + 3)^2 = 6^2$
    (i) $C(5, -3)$.
    (ii) $r = 6$.

    (b)

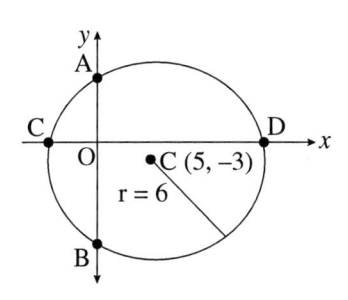

    When $x = 0$, $(y + 3)^2 = 6^2 - 25 = 36 - 25 = 11$
    $y + 3 = \pm\sqrt{11}$
    $y = -3 + \sqrt{11}, \quad y = -3 - \sqrt{11}$.
    $\therefore A(0, -3 + \sqrt{11}), \quad B(0, -3 - \sqrt{11})$.
    When $y = 0$, $(x - 5)^2 = 36 - 9 = 27$
    $x = 5 \pm \sqrt{27} = 5 \pm 3\sqrt{3}$.
    $\therefore C(5 - 3\sqrt{3}, 0), \quad D(5 + 3\sqrt{3}, 0)$.

3. (a) (i) $T_n = ar^{n-1}$
$$= 1 \times \left(\frac{1}{5}\right)^{n-1} = \frac{1}{5^{n-1}}.$$

(ii) $S_\infty = \dfrac{a}{1-r} = \dfrac{1}{1-\frac{1}{5}} = \dfrac{1}{\frac{4}{5}} = \dfrac{5}{4}.$

(b) (iii) $a, ar, ar^2, \ldots ar^{n-1}$

the third term is ar^2, the power is one less than 3 hence the nth term is one less than n, hence $T_n = ar^{n-1}$.

(iv) $S_n = a + ar + ar^2 + \ldots + ar^n$ ...(2)

multiply both sides by r ✓

$rS_n = ar + ar^2 + ar^2 + \ldots + ar^{n-1}$ ...(2)

Equation (1) minus equation (2)

$S_n - rS_n = a + ar + ar^2 + \ldots + ar^{n-1} - (ar + ar^2 + ar^3 + \ldots ar^n)$

$S_n(1-r) = a - ar^n = a(1-r^n)$

$\therefore S_n = \dfrac{a(1-r^n)}{1-r}$

or a convergent series $|r| < 1$

$\therefore |r|^\infty \to 0$

$\therefore \boxed{S_\infty = \dfrac{a}{1-r}}$

4. (a) $(2+3x)^5 = 32 + 5(2^4)(3x) + \dfrac{5 \times 4}{1 \times 2} \times 2^3(3x)^2 + \dfrac{5 \times 4 \times 3}{1 \times 2 \times 3} \times 2^2(3x)^3$

$+ \dfrac{5 \times 4 \times 3 \times 2}{1 \times 2 \times 3 \times 4} \times 2^1 \times (3x)^4 + (3x)^5$

$= 32 + 80 \times 3x + 80 \times 9x^2 + 10 \times 4 \times 27x^3$
$+ 5 \times 2 \times 81x^4 + 243x^5$

$= 32 + 240x + 720x^2 + 1080x^3 + 810x^4 + 243x^5$

$a = 32, b = 240, c = 720, d = 1080, e = 810, f = 243.$

(b) $n! = 1 \times 2 \times 3 \times \ldots \times (n-2)(n-1)n \ldots (1)$

$\begin{pmatrix} n \\ r \end{pmatrix} = {}^nC_r = \dfrac{n!}{(n-r)!r!} \quad \ldots (1)$

From (1) $n! = (n-1)!n$

if $n = 1$, $1! = (1-1)!1$

$1! = 0!$

$1 = 0!$

$\therefore 0! = 1$ (unity)

$\begin{pmatrix} 5 \\ 3 \end{pmatrix} = \dfrac{5!}{(5-3)!3!} = \dfrac{1 \times 2 \times 3 \times 4 \times 5}{1 \times 2 \times 1 \times 2 \times 3} = 10.$

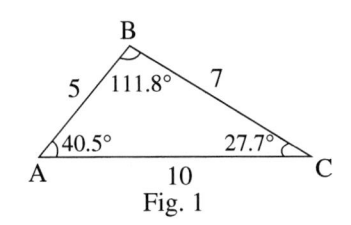

5.

Fig. 1

(Triangle ABC with AB = 5, BC = 7, AC = 10, angle A = 40.5°, angle B = 111.8°, angle C = 27.7°)

Using the cosine rule $7^2 = 5^2 + 10^2 - 2 \times 5 \times 10 \cos A$

$49 = 25 + 100 - 100 \cos A$

$100 \cos \hat{A} = 125 - 49$

$\cos \hat{A} = \dfrac{76}{100} = 0.76$

$\cos \hat{A} = 40.53580211°$

$\hat{A} = 40.5°$ to 3 s.f.

$\dfrac{7}{\sin \hat{A}} = \dfrac{5}{\sin \hat{C}} = \dfrac{10}{\sin \hat{B}}$ the sine rule

$\sin \hat{B} = \dfrac{10 \sin \hat{A}}{7}$

$= \dfrac{10 \times \sin 40.53580211°}{7}$

$= 0.928461532$

$\hat{B} = 68.19625201°$ or $111.803748°$

$\hat{B} = 68.2°$ or $111.8°$

$\sin \hat{C} = \dfrac{5 \sin A}{7} = \dfrac{5 \times \sin 40.33580211°}{7}$

$= 0.464230766$

$\hat{C} = 27.66044989°$

$= 27.7°$ to 3 s.f.

$40.5° + 111.8° + 27.7° = 180°$.

6. (a) $y = \log_a N$

by definition of logarithm

$a^y = N$

Taking logarithms on both sides to the base b

$\log_b a^y = \log_b N$

$y \log_b a = \log_b N$

$$y = \frac{\log_b N}{\log_b a}$$

$$\therefore \log_a N = \frac{\log_b N}{\log_b a}.$$

(b) $\log_6 5 = \dfrac{\log_{10} 5}{\log_{10} 6} = \dfrac{0.698910004}{0.77815125}$

$= 0.898244401.$

(c)

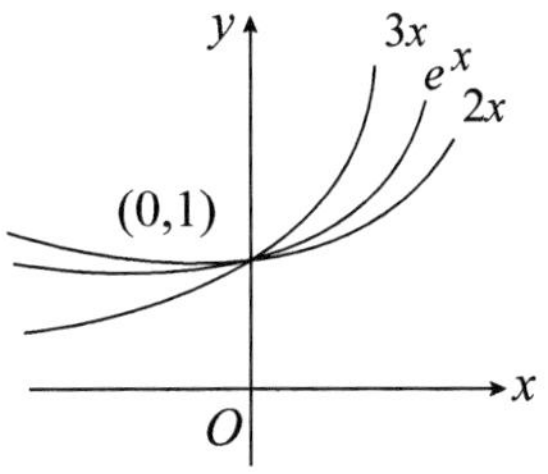

7. $y = \dfrac{1}{x^2} = 1 \Rightarrow x = \pm 1$

$y = \dfrac{1}{x^2} = 3 \Rightarrow x^2 = \dfrac{1}{3} \Rightarrow x = \pm \dfrac{1}{\sqrt{3}}$

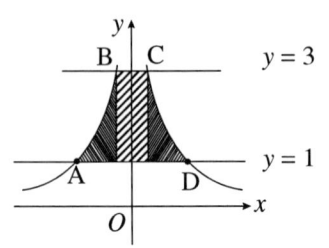

$A(-1, 1)$, $D(1, 1)$, $B\left(-\dfrac{1}{\sqrt{3}}, 3\right)$, $C\left(\dfrac{1}{\sqrt{3}}, 3\right)$

The dark shaded area is given

$\displaystyle\int_{\frac{1}{\sqrt{3}}}^{1} y\, dx = \int_{\frac{1}{\sqrt{3}}}^{1} \dfrac{1}{x^2} dx = \int_{\frac{1}{\sqrt{3}}}^{1} x^{-2} dx = \left[\dfrac{x^{-1}}{-1}\right]_{\frac{1}{\sqrt{3}}}^{1}$

$= \left(\dfrac{1}{x}\right)_{\frac{1}{\sqrt{3}}}^{1} = -\dfrac{1}{1} - \left(-\dfrac{1}{\frac{1}{\sqrt{3}}}\right) = \sqrt{3} - 1.$

The light shaded area is given

$x = 1 - \dfrac{1}{\sqrt{3}} \qquad y = 2$

$2 \times \dfrac{1}{\sqrt{3}} \times (3 - 1) = \dfrac{4}{\sqrt{3}}$

Total shaded area $= \dfrac{4}{\sqrt{3}} + 2(\sqrt{3} - 1) = 2\left(1 - \dfrac{1}{\sqrt{3}}\right)$

$= \dfrac{4}{\sqrt{3}} + 2\sqrt{3} - 2 - 2 + \dfrac{2}{\sqrt{3}}$

$= \dfrac{6}{\sqrt{3}} + 2\sqrt{3} - 4$

$= 2\sqrt{3} + 2\sqrt{3} - 4 = 4(\sqrt{3} - 1).$

8. (i) $f(x) = x^3 + 2x^2 - 5x - 6$
$f'(x) = 3x^2 + 4x - 5$
$f''(x) = 6x + 4.$

(ii) For turning points, $f'(x) = 0$
$3x^2 + 4x - 5 = 0$
$x = \dfrac{-4 \pm \sqrt{16 - 4 \times 3 \times (-5)}}{6}$
$x = \dfrac{-4 \pm \sqrt{76}}{6}.$
$x = \dfrac{-4 + \sqrt{76}}{6}$ or $x = \dfrac{-4 - \sqrt{76}}{6}$
$= 0.786$ to 3 s.f. or $= -2.12$ to 3 s.f.
$f''(x) = 6x + 4$
$f''(0.786) = 6 \times 0.786 + 4$
$ = 8.72 > 0$

minimum

$f''(-2.12) = -8.72 < 0$

maximum

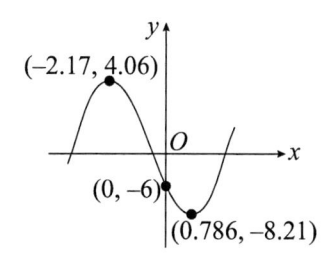

$f(-2.12) = 4.06, f(0.786) = -8.21.$

9. (i) $s = 2\pi r \dfrac{\theta^c}{2\pi} = r\theta^c =$ length of arc.

(ii) Area of sector $= \pi r^2 \times \dfrac{\theta^c}{2\pi}$

$$= \dfrac{1}{2} r^2 \theta^c.$$

$\theta°$	θ^c
0	0
30	$\dfrac{\pi}{6}$
45	$\dfrac{\pi}{4}$
60	$\dfrac{\pi}{3}$
90	$\dfrac{\pi}{2}$
120	$\dfrac{2\pi}{3}$
135	$\dfrac{3\pi}{4}$
150	$\dfrac{5\pi}{6}$
180	π
210	$\dfrac{7\pi}{6}$
225	$\dfrac{5\pi}{4}$
240	$\dfrac{4\pi}{3}$
270	$\dfrac{3\pi}{2}$
300	$\dfrac{5\pi}{3}$
315	$\dfrac{7\pi}{4}$
330	$\dfrac{11\pi}{6}$
360	2π.

TOTAL FOR PAPER: 75 MARKS